MW01108396

WisdomQuest

Volume One

STUDENT EDITION

Authors

Dr. Sharon R. Berry, Darlene Troxel and Dean Ortner

LifeWay®
Christian Resources

Published by
LifeWay Christian School Resources
Nashville, Tennessee

Created and Developed by

Christian Academic Publications and Services, Inc.
Birmingham, Alabama

ISBN: 0-6330-1001-4
Dewey Decimal Classification: 248.82
Subject Heading: CHRISTIAN LIFE--TEXTS \ BIBLE--TEXTS

No portion of this book may be reproduced in any way without the written permission of the publisher, except for brief excerpts in reviews, etc.

WisdomQuest, Volume One: Student Edition

© 2001, Christian Academic Publications and Services, Inc.
All rights reserved.

To order additional copies of this resource: WRITE LifeWay Church Resources Customer Service, 127 Ninth Avenue, North, Nashville, TN 37234-0113; FAX order to (615) 251-5933; PHONE 1-800-458-2772; EMAIL to CustomerService@Lifeway.com.

WisdomQuest

Table of Contents

Scripture quotations not otherwise marked are taken
from the *New King James Version*.
Copyright © 1982 by Thomas Nelson, Inc.
Used by permission. All rights reserved.

Scripture quotations marked (KJV) are from
The Holy Bible, King James Version.

Scripture quotations marked (NIV) are from
The Holy Bible, New International Version.
Copyright © 1978 by New York International Bible Society.
Used by permission of the Zondervan Bible Publishers.

Scripture quotations marked (NASB) are taken from
The New American Standard Bible.
Copyright © The Lockman Foundation, 1960, 1962, 1963, 1968,
1971, 1972, 1973, 1975, 1977, 1995.
Used by permission.

Scripture quotations marked (TLB) are taken from
The Living Bible
Copyright © 1971 by Tyndale House Publishers.
Used by permission. All rights reserved.

WisdomQuest
Introduction

Have you ever wondered what it would be like to live in another place and time? What if you had lived at the time of the dinosaurs, or while Pharaohs were building the pyramids? How about being a cabin boy when Columbus discovered America or riding with Wild Bill Hickok through the new frontier? Or perhaps you'd prefer the future with its intergalactic travel at the speed of light!

Whether a person lived four thousand years ago or lives four thousand years from today, their quest for wisdom would be the same. It's true that knowledge changes. What people could know even one hundred years in the past is very different from today. In the same way, what we know today may be obsolete, or not needed, tomorrow. But the need for wisdom is ageless. Throughout time people have wanted and needed to know God and how to be rightly related to Him. They have needed to know what things are most important, how to make good choices, how to get along with others, and what will happen in the future. These are questions of wisdom, and they are the topics for your study this year.

Each week you will consider one of the greatest passages of the Bible. You will use various Bible study methods to glean its truths and then make application to your own life. Students your age are growing and changing physically. They are also changing in the way they can think for themselves and make wise, considered choices. For that reason your challenge is to go beyond just enjoying a good Bible story to actually studying Scripture yourself and then using the principles to help you make decisions about life.

At the same time, you will share the experiences of Cadets Cody, Jennifer and Andrew on their quest to find their parents who have been kidnapped by space pirates. While the scene is set far into the future, their challenges of learning and using wisdom are the same as yours. Each week you will follow their travels as you consider five elements of wisdom:

Knowing God
Believing His Word
Renewing the Mind with God's Truth
Responding to Others with a Christ-like Attitude
Being Willing to Serve the Lord by Meeting the Needs
   of Others

Additionally, you will complete various Cadet Challenges as you develop your Bible studies. Your teacher has many exciting activities planned for you. Like all *QUEST* courses which balance between information and application, you can expect many opportunities to relate what you learn to real-life situations. You can also expect lots of opportunities to share what you are learning with your friends.

The purpose of the course is that you will learn to study God's words and works for yourself. Then, from that knowledge, you will grow in wisdom. May you be blessed as you begin your own *WisdomQuest*.

> *"That the God of our Lord Jesus Christ, the Father of glory, may give to you the spirit of wisdom and revelation in the knowledge of Him—in whom are hidden all the treasures of wisdom and knowledge."*
>
> (Ephesians 1:17 and Colossians 2:3)

Wisdom Is . . .

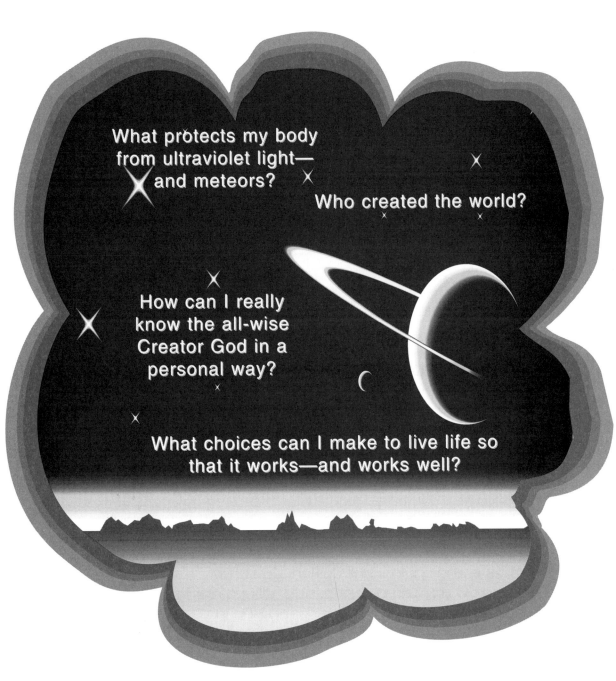

What protects my body from ultraviolet light—and meteors?

Who created the world?

How can I really know the all-wise Creator God in a personal way?

What choices can I make to live life so that it works—and works well?

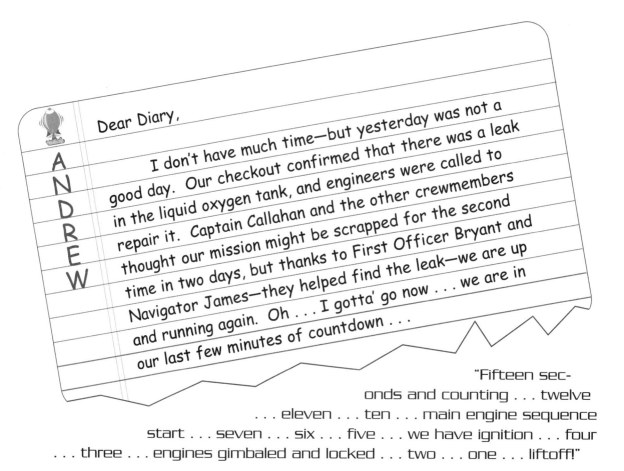

Dear Diary,

I don't have much time—but yesterday was not a good day. Our checkout confirmed that there was a leak in the liquid oxygen tank, and engineers were called to repair it. Captain Callahan and the other crewmembers thought our mission might be scrapped for the second time in two days, but thanks to First Officer Bryant and Navigator James—they helped find the leak—we are up and running again. Oh . . . I gotta' go now . . . we are in our last few minutes of countdown . . .

"Fifteen seconds and counting . . . twelve . . . eleven . . . ten . . . main engine sequence start . . . seven . . . six . . . five . . . we have ignition . . . four . . . three . . . engines gimbaled and locked . . . two . . . one . . . liftoff!"

"Roger that, CAP COM, we're steady at 90 percent power, awaiting your mark to increase to 104 percent," stated Captain Callahan. The thunderous roar was felt as much as heard throughout the ship. Even with helmets on, the sound was almost unbearable.

"What—I can't hear you," shouted Andrew to Cody. "Let me turn up my volume."

"I said, is Captain Callahan positive that the ship's hull can withstand the power of these new engines?" Cody asked, concerned.

"This is the original hull design, you know. It will be fine, Cody. Relax!" Andrew answered confidently. "Good engineers always design extra safeties, especially for systems used in the space program—except when they are trying to save money. If they know their facts and the limitations of the materials used, then there is no problem. They could probably go to 10 percent over the designed power limit and still be fine."

All of a sudden there was silence—no sound at all. The three cadets looked at each other without saying a word. "The . . . the engines have shut down," gasped Cody.

"Take it easy, Cody," Jennifer said. "We are just between the stages of the rocket engines. The next stage should ignite pretty soon now. In fact right about . . . ."

Boom! Boom! The crew was thrown back again into their acceleration couches. Not needing to lift the extra mass of the first stage or the extra push necessary to plow through so much atmosphere, the second stage didn't need to be as powerful. The noise wasn't as deafening this time.

"Captain! I need you to check the fuel flow to the starboard engine." Navigator James was insistent.

"Okay, keep monitoring and keep me informed," replied the Captain.

The second stage fell away and was followed by the steady drone and thrumming of the ship's main thrusters used for deep space flight. "Are . . . are we up, Captain Callahan?" Cody's voice quivered. "Are the engines still running?"

"C'mon Cody!" Andrew said sounding irritated.

"It's okay, Cody. Really!" Captain Callahan replied. "We're in sub-orbital insertion mode now and will be for awhile. It will take another half hour to reach our desired orbit. Come on over and enjoy the view."

"Captain." Navigator James motioned for the Captain to move to the far side of the cabin. "A problem has developed," James said in an urgent whisper.

Jennifer and Andrew made their way to the portal, with Cody following behind. "Wow . . . look at the curvature of the earth," said Andrew in awe.

Jennifer crowded close—and then—her eyes grew wide. "I've never seen anything so beautiful!" she exclaimed.

"Even though it's scary, it's . . . awesome," responded Cody. God's creation is . . . well . . . it's just awesome.

"What's amazing is how thin the atmospheric layer is," commented Andrew. "Just look at that little thin, hazy blue line just above the surface."

"That little thin, hazy blue line is what keeps you alive, my young friends," interjected First Officer Bryant as he peeked out the portal. "It shields Earth from meteors by causing most of them to burn up before they can hit the ground. The upper ozone layer blocks the dangerous ultraviolet rays. The atmospheric pressure allows the right amount of oxygen to reach our bloodstream, and even that blue color is important to our survival. In fact, the ecosystem of Earth is of far more complex design than even the design of this spacecraft. There must have been hundreds of engineers working on this ship for several years. Just imagine the wisdom of the Creator in putting together such a marvelous world in just seven days."

"Captain," Navigator James cautioned as he wrinkled his brow, "those flow rates are not within parameters. If the signals coming from the fuel flow sensors are valid, then we could be off course and you'll need to recompute our trajectory immediately. If this continues, our mission could be jeopardized and the ship in danger."

With expert and experienced hands, the Captain adjusted the thrust vectors. Drawing from his years of training, he computed what had to be done to correct the problem and then quickly acted on that information to save the ship.

"That was some amazing piloting, Captain," said Andrew. "I guess it's not enough to just KNOW facts—like my teacher said—you have to actually use the facts to make the right decisions—decisions that work."

"Yep," said Navigator James. "Captain is full of wisdom alright."

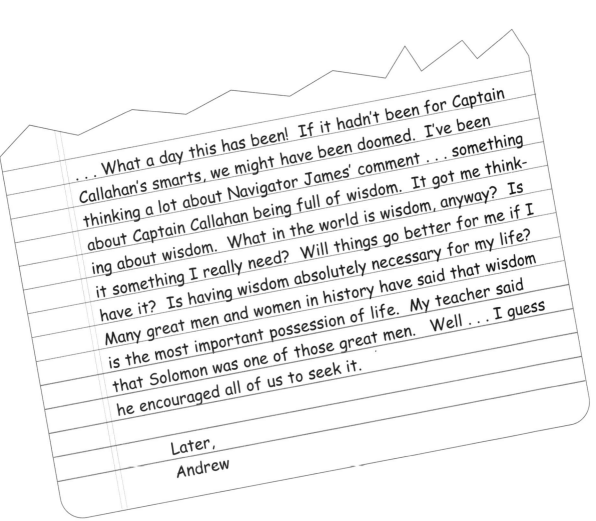

. . . What a day this has been! If it hadn't been for Captain Callahan's smarts, we might have been doomed. I've been thinking a lot about Navigator James' comment . . . something about Captain Callahan being full of wisdom. It got me thinking about wisdom. What in the world is wisdom, anyway? Is it something I really need? Will things go better for me if I have it? Is having wisdom absolutely necessary for my life? Many great men and women in history have said that wisdom is the most important possession of life. My teacher said that Solomon was one of those great men. Well . . . I guess he encouraged all of us to seek it.

Later,
Andrew

In Proverbs 4:7 Solomon said, "Wisdom is the principal thing; therefore get wisdom. And in all your getting, get understanding."

How about you? If Solomon is right, then how do you get this wisdom? Are you born with it? Did your family pass it on to you? Or did you get it from going to school or church? To answer these questions, think about some of the characteristics of wise people. What are they like? What is important to them? How do they choose to act? From the list below, think about the ones that best describe a person who has wisdom.

A wise person . . .

- ☐ does well in school.
- ☑ knows God.
- ☐ is a good athlete.
- ☐ gets up early.
- ☑ believes in God's Word.
- ☑ takes care of their room.
- ☑ renews their mind with God's truth.
- ☑ responds to others with a Christ-like attitude.

- ☐ never fails at anything.
- ☐ goes to the mission field.
- ☐ doesn't talk on the phone.
- ☐ gives all money to the poor.
- ☐ is popular with friends.
- ☑ is willing to serve the Lord.
- ☐ has lots of money.
- ☐ is interested in a hobby.
- ☐ feeds the family pets.

In Bible class this year, you will study the topic of wisdom. You might be asking, how in the world does knowing God, believing in His Word, renewing your mind, responding to others and being willing to serve relate to the topic of wisdom? That is exactly what you are about to discover. The following web gives you an outline for our exciting mission, our *WisdomQuest*.

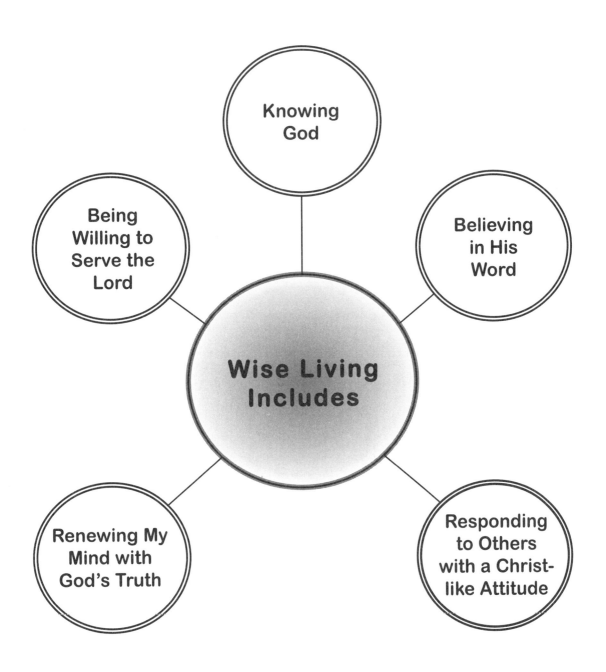

Knowing God

Being Willing to Serve the Lord

Believing in His Word

Wise Living Includes

Renewing My Mind with God's Truth

Responding to Others with a Christ-like Attitude

Cadet Challenge 1.1

Proverbs 4:4-7 [NKJV]

Write the verses by replacing all the vowels, capital letters and puctuation marks.

h l s t g h t m n d s d t m l t y r h r t r t n m y w r d s
k p m y c m m n d s n d l v t w s d m t n d r s t n d n g
d n t f r g t n r t r n w y f r m t h w r d s f m y m t h
d n t f r s k h r n d s h w l l p r s r v y l v h r n d s h w l l k p y
w s d m s t h p r n c p l t h n g t h r f r g t w s d m
n d n l l y r g t t n g g t n d r s t n d n g

He also taught me and said to me
get your heart retain my words and
keep my command and live, get wisdom
get understanding do not forget nor
turn away from the words of my mouth,
to not forsake her and she will preserve
you love her and she will keep you
wisdom is the principle thing
get wisdom and in all your getting get
understanding.

Cadet Challenge 1.2

Wisdom—Am I Getting It?

In the five categories, check the items that are true if you are getting wisom.

1. I am growing in **KNOWING GOD**.
   - ___✓___ I understand that I am a sinner.
   - ___✓___ I believe that God is holy.
   - ___✓___ I have trusted in Jesus Christ, God's Son, as my personal Savior.
   - _____ I read my Bible on a regular basis.
   - ___✓___ I pray to God often.

2. I am growing by **BELIEVING GOD'S WORD**.
   - ___✓___ I believe that God's Word is true.
   - ___✓___ I believe that God created the world and everything in it.
   - ___✓___ I am trusting in God's faithfulness in my life.
   - ___✓___ I believe God's Word helps me know how to live to please God.
   - _____ I am learning to make good choices as I read or hear God's Word.

3. I am growing by **RENEWING MY MIND**.
   - ___✓___ I confess my sins to God daily.
   - ___✓___ I apologize to my parents when I do not obey them.
   - ___✓___ I desire to have pure thoughts.
   - _____ I feel badly when I read something in the Bible that points out my sins.
   - _____ I am saying no to my friends when they encourage me to do wrong things.

4. I am growing by **RESPONDING TO OTHERS** with love and kind actions.
   - ___✓___ I do not make fun of others.
   - _____ I treat others with fairness and do not gang up on them.
   - ___✓___ I make myself friendly to my peers.
   - ___✓___ I encourage my friends when they are going a through hard time.
   - ___✓___ I respond to the needy by giving my time or part of my allowance to help.

5. I am growing in being **WILLING TO SERVE THE LORD**.
   - ___✓___ I go to church without complaining.
   - _____ I volunteer for special projects or ministries in the church.
   - ___✓___ I feel it is important to give part of my allowance to church.
   - _____ I willingly obey my parents when they ask me to do chores at home.
   - ___✓___ I tell others about how to become a Christian.

15

Fearing God

What makes you afraid?

What is the fear of the Lord?

Who is the Lord that you should fear Him?

How does fearing the Lord benefit you?

A N D R E W

Dear Diary,

Yesterday was a big day! We had liftoff with only a few scary moments, thanks to Captain Callahan and his knowledge and experience. He steered us back on course. He is a very wise man—and boy, are the rest of us glad. Officer Bryant says that Captain is the most respected . . . oh . . . hang on . . . gotta' go. Navigator James wants us to be oriented or something . . . .

"That last burn put us right on the numbers, Captain," said Navigator James. "We won't be coming up on the next maneuver for another orbit, so I might as well give some orientation to our young cadets."

"Okay, crewmember wannabes," he quipped, rapping Cody and Jennifer on their helmets, "out of those acceleration couches and follow me. You too, Andrew."

"I'd rather stay here if you don't mind, sir," said Cody. "I . . . I think it is safer."

"Just a minute—I'm in the shower," Jennifer teased after Navigator James rapped on her helmet a second time.

Without the crushing pressure pushing him into the acceleration couch, Andrew was out and already standing alongside the officer. The first thing he grabbed was his space diary, eager to document their experiences.

"Do . . . do we have to leave this cabin?" asked Cody. "I think I need to get used to space again."

"That will come with time—and very quickly," replied James. "I want you to spend some time with First Officer Bryant since you will be working closely with him."

"Officer Bryant, meet your Cadets, Andrew, Jennifer and Cody. They are here for your orientation so they can learn about the operation of this ship. Some kind of an experimental program, I'm told."

"Hello Cadets, and welcome aboard." First Officer Bryant seemed friendlier than Navigator James. The cadets would enjoy working with him.

"They're all yours, Officer Bryant. I've got to get back to the deck and prepare for our docking with Orion. If you haven't seen the new space station yet, you're in for quite an experience."

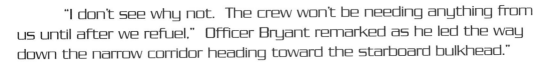

"Come on Cody, let's go to the observation deck and watch," encouraged Andrew, hoping to distract him from his initial space sickness . . . and his fear. "Do you think it's okay, Officer Bryant?" he asked.

"I don't see why not. The crew won't be needing anything from us until after we refuel," Officer Bryant remarked as he led the way down the narrow corridor heading toward the starboard bulkhead."

"Jennifer, look!" Andrew exclaimed. "It's like a picture window into space."

"It's a new material we're testing for surface abrasion resistance," said Officer Bryant. "The old primitive shuttles had only small triangular peek holes barely big enough for one person's head. With this view, the immensity of God's handiwork will take your breath away."

The Cadets were awestruck. They gazed at the black velvet of cold space. The tiny points of light were actually raging nuclear "star furnaces," but from this distance they disguised themselves as diamond dust. They were no longer twinkling now, viewed above the earth's atmosphere, but still beckoning.

Cody looked around and relaxed a bit. "And to think the Creator knows each star by name! What an awesome Designer!"

"What an awesome Creator!" Jennifer exclaimed.

"You can say that again," Andrew replied. "You can see why Captain Callahan keeps reminding us that God is the all-wise, all-powerful, all-knowing God."

"Can we visit the Captain, Officer Bryant?" Cody asked. "We want to see what his view is like."

"Whoa! I think we need to go over some protocol, Cadets," Bryant remarked in an official sounding way. "While you may be friends with Captain Callahan off this ship, he is the Captain onboard and his word is absolute law here. You don't approach him without an escort, you don't speak unless spoken to first and you don't ever enter the bridge without being summoned, and even then we'll escort you. You show respect and obey the rules. Is that understood?"

They all swallowed hard and nodded.

"I can't hear you, Cadets." Officer Bryant's voice was more thunderous with each syllable.

"Yes sir!" They all answered in unison, relieved when he smiled.

Andrew and Jennifer both recalled the time Captain Callahan had escorted them around the launch facility in their first year of training for this mission. They were so proud to be considered his friends as they watched roomfulls of personnel stand to attention when he walked in. Everyone respected him, and no one wanted to disappoint him.

Up on the bridge things were busy now that the docking phase was approaching. Officer James had his capable hands quite full.

"Ease up a bit on number two thruster, James. I want to take us in a bit slower than the book calls for," Captain Callahan said.

"Roger, Captain, I need to watch that fuel flow pretty carefully anyway," James replied as he monitored systems. "We had a bit of a scare back there during launch, didn't we?"

"Could have been touch and go for awhile if we hadn't compensated," Captain Callahan confessed. "I'll recommend engineering changes when we get back." It was a tremendous responsibility overseeing the command of a ship. It would require total commitment and respect from the entire crew if they were going to pull off this
mission successfully. Not even his officers, or the cadets, knew the total reason, nor did they fully realize how critical it would be
for the whole crew, including the cadets, to trust
him and to do their jobs well.

. . . I'm back, finally. But it's about time to rotate sleeps, so I don't have much time since mine comes first. Ugh! I'd rather be up watching TV, but those are the Captain's orders.

Jennifer's great—even if she is a girl. But Cody . . . well, I wish Cody would settle down. He's still fearful—of just about everything. And to tell you the truth, sometimes he gets on my nerves. Today, though, he didn't seem to question the Captain as much—so that's good. I think maybe Cody's beginning to trust him more—and who wouldn't? Captain Callahan seems to know everything about . . . oops . . . the Captain's calling me.

Signing off,

Andrew

P.S. The Captain really cares about our safety, too. I'm learning to respect him a whole lot.

Andrew and the rest of the crew are growing in their respect for Captain Callahan—but who do you respect? Your father and your mother? Maybe a special teacher or a distant relative? What makes you respect people? What character qualities do they have? Are they intelligent, handsome, witty or wise? Do they treat others with respect? Do they have good attitudes? Check the top three character qualities, actions or attitudes of the people that you most respect.

☐ shows kindness	☐ acts proud	☑ prays often
☐ truthful	☐ integrity	☐ loves unconditionally
☑ intelligent	☐ attentive	☐ positive
☐ fair	☐ thoughtful	☐ witty
☐ generous	☐ beautiful/handsome	☐ respects others
☑ loving	☐ friendly	☐ wise

Now, think again of the people that you respect the most, and ask yourself the following questions: Do you believe them when they talk? Do you listen to what they say? Do you take their advice—do you obey them? Does it bother you to think you might disappoint or displease them with your speech or actions? When you are around them, are you on your best behavior? Does your respect for them keep you from doing the wrong things? Do they benefit your life in some way?

If you answered yes to the questions above, then the way you respond to the people that you respect is similar to the way God wants us to respond to Him as we learn to fear the Lord. When we truly fear the Lord, we will have a healthy respect for Him that is demonstrated by our actions and attitude toward Him. We will believe what He says in His Word. We will want to obey because we have respect for His awesome power. We will not want to displease Him, because of the unconditional love He has shown toward us.

This week you will study what the fear of the Lord is and how important it is. You will also see how having the proper fear of the Lord benefits your life and keeps you from suffering the consequences of making wrong decisions. God wants you to grow in your respect for your Creator God.

Cadet Challenge 2.1

Revelation 15:4

Fill in the words to complete the verse.

"Who shall not _fear_ _you_.

O Lord, and _glorify_ _youre_

name? For _you_ alone are

holy. For all _nations_ shall

come and _worship_ before

you."

Cadet Challenge 2.2

═Who is the Lord that you should fear Him?═

Read Isaiah 40:6–31 and write some of the reasons you should fear God.

were grass compared to God

verses 6–8

God will not fail

verses 18–20

God created everything

verses 9–11

we are grasshopper compared to God

verses 21–24

he knows everything

verses 12–14

he knows stars by name

verses 25–26

God is bigger than anything

verses 15–17

God is everlasting

verses 27–31

Cadet Challenge 2.3

To Fear God Is to Respect Him

On the chart write the actions that demonstrate a lack of respect for God and then actions which demonstrate respect for God. Then write a statement in the space below which illustrates your commitment to fearing God.

I am fearing God when I ....

I am _not_ fearing God when I . . .

MY COMMITMENT

Believing God's Word

When do you have trouble believing that something will really come true?

How do people who believe God's Word act?

What are some of the reasons people do not believe God?

How is believing God's Word related to wisdom?

CODY

Dear Diary,

Nothing too much is going on up here today—just routine stuff. Devotions this morning were about Noah and the ark. What a story! He was really a man of faith! I keep hearing Officer Bryant asking questions about "the cadets." He doesn't seem to know why we are here yet. I'm just glad Captain Callahan made a way for us to come. I don't know what we would've done—we would've been doomed if . . .

"You know, Captain Callahan, the Academy taught me to follow orders, sir." Officer Bryant finally remarked after a long silence.

"I realize those cadets are our responsibility for now, but right before we docked with Orion to re-fuel, you seemed to imply that more is in store for them once we reach our undisclosed destination. I sure wonder what they've gotten themselves into."

"I'm not at liberty to discuss it. You should know that," the Captain said sternly. Actually, he'd been wondering the same thing.

Officer Bryant rubbed his cheek. "Yes sir, I realize that. I'm not pressing for any classified information; I'd end up in the brig! What I wondered about was how could such a young crew have the maturity to completely trust their superiors by blind faith? Your sterling reputation and record of accomplishments convince me to follow you, but they know little about those of us who are directing their destiny."

The captain swirled his juice while watching the unusual fluid patterns around the cup's rim, caused by the minimal gravity condition of the station. He'd periodically glanced at his remote instrumentation clipboard. That convenient device showed the status of the ship's control console indicators. At last, no more waiting on board the ship to monitor systems. Now he could "take the ship with him" and maintain constant contact.

"Captain? Are you okay?" Bryant asked hesitantly. He'd rarely seen him so quiet and reflective.

"Sorry, Officer Bryant. I was just thinking about when their parents were set adrift and I became their temporary guardian. I assumed it would be for only a short time, but then we lost contact with the ship somewhere in the asteroid belt. I've kind of adopted them. They've really taken to space travel. They work like naturals. It's no wonder they've been sent on this mission. I can tell you that even as young as they are, they've been training for years. That's public knowledge."

Just then the remote console beeped, alerting him that the tanks were near their capacity. Getting up to leave, Captain Callahan said, "I will tell you this, Bryant, you and your navi-gator friend, James, have the singular responsibility to put the finishing touches on their training. The cadets have learned to totally trust their coaches and instructors for the things they don't understand or can't be told yet. That's the way it is with trust and faith. If you've never been let down in the past, if you've never been disappointed in what or in whom you trust, then it's easier to have faith to press on in spite of the unknowns."

Meanwhile, back in the "tank farm," Cody was finally relaxing—and laughing his head off while listening to the special high-energy fuel flow into the auxiliary tanks.

"Hey you guys, listen to this!" he managed to get out in between laughter. "It sounds like Jennifer's stomach when she's really hungry."

"It does not, you poor excuse for a Corellian Wombat! My stomach doesn't gurgle like that fuel moving in those pipes. Your brain's on imagination overtime and I'm not playing!" Jennifer jabbed Cody in the ribs.

"Ha, ha, didn't hurt—tickle me again," he winced, but didn't let her see that she really got him a good one.

"Cody, Jennifer, come to this side and look at these enormous fuel tanks!" Andrew exclaimed. "It sure is great to have our Umbra Class secret clearance. We're seeing things that even the Captain's Top Secret Clearance doesn't clear him to experience."

"Roger on that one," Jennifer replied. "I wish we could tell him more. He's been so supportive since our parents disappeared."

Cody got really quiet. As the youngest, it was hardest for him to take. His whole world had come to an end, just like in the days of Noah and the flood. Everything he'd grown accustomed to was gone. Now he was drifting on a sea of unknowns. If it weren't for Captain Callahan taking them in, he wouldn't have known who to trust. But now, at least, they have a purpose, and it has so much potential and excitement that he's nearly bursting. But conversations were restricted; the three of them could only share together until after the mission's successful completion.

"Wow, look at the size of those auxiliary tanks. They're actually bigger than the main boosters that got us up here," Jennifer marveled. "When dad and mom designed this ship, they really had a long trip in mind."

"I'll say. But things always look bigger when you're standing next to them. This is so huge that it could never be built down on earth. They'd never get it up into space!" Andrew concluded. "I see why Officer James was the one to navigate us into dock. He's the best the Academy has ever graduated."

"Yeah, until you came along, Andrew. No one has ever gotten

scores as high as you except for perhaps Mom," Jennifer added proudly. "The way you and Cody do math games together is amazing."

"Well, nobody can pilot a ship in tighter formation than you can, Jen. I've seen your scores and you even topped Dad's best in the simulator. Too bad we can't tell anyone about any of this. Still, it is fun to pretend we're just a bunch of cadets. I can hardly wait to see their faces when we launch out on our own."

"The three of us are a unique team, totally trusting in each other's commitment and abilities, but we also have faith in the documents that Dad and Mom left behind," Andrew reflected. "Even though our parents aren't with us, they've always proven to be reliable in the past with what they've told us. So now we can also rely on things they said—the things they set up for the future mission."

"It's still going to be risky, but it's the only way we'll ever know what happened and the only way we have any chance of seeing them alive again," cautioned Jennifer.

"Come on you two jabberwoks, we've got some astro-plotting to finish," Cody interjected. The three of them sauntered off to their quarters, excited to be on their way at last for the trip of a lifetime.

. . . This ship is REALLY awesome—built to perfection . . . well . . . kind of like Noah's ark. So glad Mom and Dad thought of everything and glad we can trust their plans—even though they aren't here with us now. You know . . . if Captain Callahan hadn't invited us to come along . . . well . . . he saved our lives . . . . Wow! This really does sound like the flood—Noah and his ark . . . although there are only six of us . . . but then again . . . if Mom and Dad were here . . . there would be eight of us. Wow!

Later,

Cody

The flood of Noah and his ark? You might be thinking—that story is better for preschoolers. But did you know that for years the flood of Noah and his ark has been a topic of conversation among Christians and non-Christians alike? In recent years a multitude of adventurers have risked their lives exploring steep terrains to find evidence of it. And why? The Bible gives the answers.

For Christians, the flood of Noah is an event that happened just as God said it would. It is an example of His judgment poured out on all those who were unrighteous. All living things who did not believe His Word and take shelter in the ark perished. Not only does the ark speak of God's judgment, but it is also a picture of God's grace toward a righteous family of eight who believed what God said He would do. Noah, his wife, his sons and their wives simply trusted that God was telling the truth, obeyed Him and took refuge in the ark. They were the only survivors—the only ones left in the world to receive God's blessings.

Do not be surprised when you run across modern-day Bible skeptics. Who are they? Like the people in Noah's day, they are ones who mock his simple faith and trust in God. They are the ones who do not believe in God's Word. They are the ones who use all means to discredit the Biblical accounts, especially those of God's Son, God's Creation and the flood of Noah. The Apostle Peter anticipated that people in our day would doubt the flood of Noah; he wrote about it in 2 Peter 3. This week you will be amazed to find out things you did not know about Noah, the flood, the ark and what God predicted long ago. Like the Cadets, you will see Noah's faith as a picture of our salvation.

Cadet Challenge 3.1

Hebrews 11:6

Complete each word of the verse.

"B ut w ithout f aith it is
i mpossible to p lease H im,
for h e who c omes to G od
m ust b elive that He is,
and t hat He is a r ewarder
of t those who d ignently
s eek H im."

Cadet Challenge 3.2

What Was Noah Like?

Write a fact from each reference.

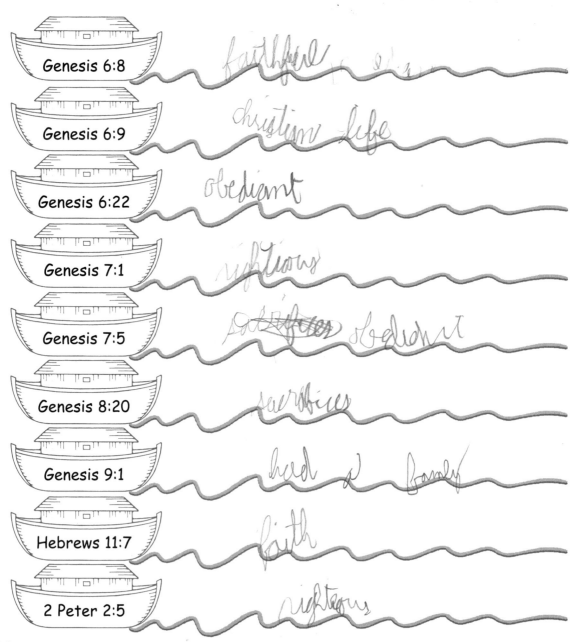

Genesis 6:8 — faithful

Genesis 6:9 — christian life

Genesis 6:22 — obedient

Genesis 7:1 — righteous

Genesis 7:5 — sacrifices obedient

Genesis 8:20 — sacrifices

Genesis 9:1 — had a family

Hebrews 11:7 — faith

2 Peter 2:5 — righteous

Acting in Faith

What is faith?

Does everyone have faith?

What should be the object of my faith?

How do people behave when they have faith?

What is the difference between blind faith and real faith?

Dear Diary,

A
N
D
R
E
W

Just ate breakfast . . . or that's what Navigator James said it was. I don't mean to complain, but it tasted more like wet cardboard to me. This extraterrestrial food is not—well—it's not like Mom's.

I like Officer Bryant, but sometimes he's hard to understand. Take this morning for example. He said something to the cadets about we shouldn't have blind faith—and I had no idea what in the world he was talking about—I don't think Cody did either. Jen seemed to understand, so maybe I'll ask her . . . . . . oh no . . . something must have happened to . . . later!

"Andrew!" Jennifer yelled in a startled voice. "What was that?"

"Cody, did you feel it too?" Andrew asked with concern. "It felt like a shudder in the deck plates."

"Yes, I did feel it and I don't like it one bit!" Cody said. "What was it?"

"The force of that vibration either means a minor pressure rupture nearby or something really serious on the far side of the station. That's near the fuel storage area where we just left the Captain," Jennifer said. "I hope nothing's gone . . . ."

Wham! They were thrown to their stomachs as the PTT (Personnel Transport Tube) slammed against the side of the outer hull. The bright flash of the white-hot gaseous flame would have temporarily blinded them had they not been thrown face down on the deck.

"Ouch, my nose is bleeding!" yelled Cody.

"Come on you two!" insisted Andrew. "We've got to scramble out of this tube before the seams rupture and we're breathing space!"

Jennifer and Andrew each grabbed one of Cody's arms and dragged him past the main coupling and into one of the main spokes. The spokes connected the central hub of the space station Orion with its three outer wheels. The many PTT's inter-linking the whole system made the station look like a giant spider web.

"Th . . . th . . . thanks you guys, I think," Cody managed to get out between gasps for air. "What was that anyway?" he exclaimed. Cody had always had total faith in his family to take care of him if he ever needed rescuing. Now was was one of those times.

"I'm not sure, but I think we've had a major incident on one of the outer wheel sections," Andrew said, trying to peer around the heads of the station crew who had gathered near the viewing port.

"We get so used to everything working like it's supposed to, just like the designers planned, but sometimes that faith is misplaced. After all, they're only human. Now if God had built this ship, you could have total unreserved faith in everything! But we must remember that He didn't," mused one of the crewmen to no one in particular.

"Let's go inside to the hub's zero gravity station," suggested Jennifer. "No one likes to stay there very long, so there should be lots of room. We can see what's going on by watching the monitors. We were close enough to the real thing, and we don't need any more reminders of what it looked like," she exclaimed.

Jennifer was right—no one was there. Andrew keyed in his code clearance since no one was watching. The three Cadets entered the Central Security/Systems Integrity monitoring station. Andrew began working the controls fast.

"Uh no!" he moaned. "One whole section of the station is gone! It's still on fire. It must be those highly self-oxygenated fuels from the experimental labs. They have so much oxygen dissolved in them that the stuff can burn underwater or even out here in space!"

"That's not good at all," Jennifer winced. "If they don't get that fire out, it could spread to the next two sections—and that's just too close for comfort to where our shuttle is docked. We came in at Delta, right?" she asked.

"Yes," said Cody, "and it looks like Alpha was damaged most. I sure hope Captain Callahan and the crew were not hurt."

"We all feel that way, Cody. I'm sure they're all right," comforted Jennifer. "They would have had no reason to go that direction once the ship was fueled."

"That may be," interjected Andrew, "but I'm still going to page him on his private channel."

Jennifer and Cody waited impatiently for the link to be made.

"Andrew!" blurted Captain Callahan between gasps. "Thank goodness! You are safe! Are there others with you?"

"All cadets are here, Captain," said Andrew. "The concussion threw the three of us onto the deck plates and Cody ended up with a bloody nose, but otherwise, we are okay. We were using the PTT's to save time. What exactly happened?"

There was a catastrophic failure in one of the pressurized fuel transfer ducts. Good thing that area is mostly automated. I . . . I don't think we lost anyone," the Captain said.

"So that's what happened. At least it wasn't sabotage." Andrew mumbled. Andrew breathed a sigh of relief. He knew that some of the work his parents had pioneered was not popular with everyone on Earth.

Andrew didn't tell Captain Callahan that after the three of them had left him at the launch vehicle, they were actually in the fueling area inspecting their deep space probe. No one knew at that time about the high level Umbra Class security clearance the Cadets had. It would just make it difficult to explain—and Andrew didn't want the Captain worrying about their safety. The Cadets had been training for years to pilot a ship they only hoped existed. That faith became a reality once they saw the ship in the fuel dock. Faith had become substance. Once unseen and only hoped for, they now could actually trust in the worthiness of its designed purpose.

"Just so you're all okay, Andrew," Captain Callahan said still concerned. "You'd better contact Officer James and especially Officer Bryant. He'll be concerned since you're his responsibility. Launch may be delayed until we can make sure there's been no structural damage. We'll be flying in tandem for a major part of the mission—and these ships have to be functioning perfectly."

"You got that right, Captain—but wouldn't you say for us also to have a little faith?" Andrew teased.

The Captain chuckled. "Yes, I would. But I would also remind you, Cadet Andrew, that your faith is only as good as the object of your faith . . . . Good night, Andrew. You have a big day ahead of you tomorrow."

"Yes sir!" Andrew said. "And probably bigger ones after that!"

. . . It's me again—Cadet Andrew here. Cody and Jennifer have already turned in and I'm almost there—every bone in my body hurts after that horrible problem with the fuel transfer duct. I really thought we wouldn't make it. But . . . well—this ship is awesome—really awesome! It's still operating fine—even after the fire and all.

I think I finally know what Officer Bryant meant when he talked about blind faith. When Captain Callahan said, "Your faith is only as good as the object of your faith," it hit me. Blind faith is when you don't have a worthy object of your faith. Just as our crew has faith in the ship because it is a reliable, proven spacecraft, we should have faith because God is a worthy object. What an awesome thought! Anyway, I think I'm getting it!

Later, Andrew

Worthy object or blind faith—what's the difference? Andrew was confused, too, until the Captain made the statement, "Your faith is only as good as the object of your faith." How about you? Do you understand the importance of trusting in a worthy object, or do you sometimes find yourself operating out of a blind faith? Take a minute to evaluate yourself. To understand the differences between the two ideas, check the actions that illustrate having a blind faith and being ready to give a reason why based on true faith.

☑ 1. He jumped out of an airplane and trusted an umbrella to save him.

☐ 2. The man knew his boss would pay him because he had never before missed a paycheck.

☑ 3. The teenager took an aspirin and believed that it would cure poison ivy.

☑ 4. The woman believed that she would win a trip to Europe because she wanted to win.

☐ 5. The boy knew that his bicycle would be returned to him after forgetting it at school.

☑ 6. The girl trusted her father to come for her at school because he did every day.

Now, why is it so important to have a reliable or worthy object for your faith? Because having faith in something that is unreliable or someone who is not worthy is like having blind faith. What's the object of your faith in God? Is it your good works, your family heritage, your Christian school—or is it the most reliable and worthy object of all, the Lord Jesus Christ? Remember what the Captain said, "Your faith is only as good as the object of your faith."

Cadet Challenge 4.1

Hebrews 11:1–3

Write the correct words for the shaded words.

"Now _faith_ is the _substance_
_____ firm belief _____ evidence

of ___things___ hoped for, the
items and events

evidence of things not _seen_. For
surities experienced

by it the _elders_ obtained a _good_
Bible people

___testimony___. By _faith_
positive story about trusting God firm belief

we understand that the _worlds_ were
universes

framed by the _word_ of God, so
created speaking

that the _things_ which
objects and people

are seen were not made _things_
you now see from items

which _are visible_ ."
have appeared by themselves

Cadet Challenge 4.2

Hebrews 11 . . . the Faith Chapter

Read Hebrews 11 and write one way each person demonstrated faith in God.

Abel _good offering_

Enoch _pleased God with a good testimony_

Noah _was ritheous_

Abraham _listened to God_

Sarah _was faithful to God_

Isaac _was full of blessings_

Jacob _worshiped Him_

Joshua
You figure it out! _trusted God all the way_

Rahab _belived that God would save her_

Moses' Parents _they knew that God would keep moses safe_

Moses _____

FAITH OF OUR FOREFATHERS

42

Loving Others

How important is love?

How do we know God loves us?

How do we demonstrate God's love to others?

Is there anything I should hate?

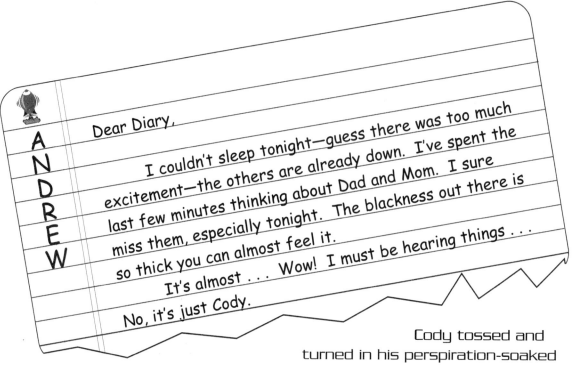

ANDREW

Dear Diary,

I couldn't sleep tonight—guess there was too much excitement—the others are already down. I've spent the last few minutes thinking about Dad and Mom. I sure miss them, especially tonight. The blackness out there is so thick you can almost feel it.

It's almost . . . Wow! I must be hearing things . . .

No, it's just Cody.

Cody tossed and turned in his perspiration-soaked pajamas. "Mom, Mom!" Cody screamed. "I can't see anymore. Where are you? I can't find Dad!" He bolted upright in bed, relieved it was only a dream.

"Jennifer! It's Cody again," whispered Andrew through his wrist COM. "He's had another nightmare." They both jumped out of their beds at the same time and rushed to meet at Cody's quarters.

"It's okay, Cody," Jennifer assured him. "You probably got scared because of that explosion last week over in Alpha Dock. It just reminds you of the accident. We're here with you, so everything is okay."

"Sorry, guys," he said sheepishly. "I hate to be such a baby."

"You may be small, but you're not a baby!" Jennifer assured him.

"Do you still love me? Well . . . I mean . . . do you?" Cody asked.

"Of course we do," Andrew said. "You know we do. Now don't get wimpy on us."

"Remember how Dad and Mom would quote 1 Corinthians 13:4 to us? 'Love suffers long and is kind.' You two have done that for me," Cody said almost in tears.

44

"Yeah, you're pretty hard to love, Cody," Andrew teased.

"You too, Jen?" Cody inquired.

"We do love you, Cody," Jen said encouragingly.

"Yep! Me too," Andrew assured Cody. "Now let's get some sleep. I'm sure they might want our help during repairs to the station. We may even need to move the probe to a different docking station. Once it comes out from under wraps, the mystery will be revealed and we'll have lots of questions to answer."

The next morning, the Cadets were awakened by the metallic sounds of the station repair robots cutting and riveting the deck plates. It was really amazing how quickly the repairs got under way. Andrew thought back to the comical days of the early Space Shuttle missions. The emergency repair kit in those days consisted of a pack of gooey silicon-ceramic material that was applied with a trowel. The areas where any heat tiles were blown off or gouged through to the shuttle's outer skin would need insulation from the heat of re-entry.

"Look at that thing go!" Jennifer exclaimed. "It takes a wide sheet of relatively thin metal and automatically folds it into beams, trusses and cross-members, then rivets them in place. Those robots look almost like an army of spiders building a giant web."

"Hey Andrew, how long have you been up?" asked Cody. "I must have slept like a meteor the rest of the night."

"I've been up since 0600, or 6 A.M. to you young Cadets," Andrew smiled.

"What do you mean, 'young cadets'? I know military and space time uses the 24-hour time system: 0900 hours is 9 a.m., 1500 hours is 3 P.M., 2200 hours is 11 P.M.," Cody shot back.

"Very good, Cody," Jennifer joined in. "So what's 1730 hours, smarty pants?"

"Uh, let's see, . . . umm . . . 5:30 in the afternoon, right?" he answered.

"Hey, imagine that, Andrew. We just might keep him as the astro-nav on the mission, if he'd only get over being so nervous about space," Jennifer quipped sarcastically.

"Knock it off, Jen. You know he's going to get used to it in another few days," said Andrew, cutting in.

"I know. I was just giving him the business for fun," she admitted as all three cadets refocused on the repair work being completed.

"It's good that those robots were able to handle the repairs without having to access the docking bay where our experimental ship is moored. Like I said last night, I don't want to have to explain to the crew why we have such a high security clearance." Andrew seemed relieved.

"I'm glad, too," replied Jennifer. "It's funny that secrets have to be kept from so many people all the time. I guess the Federation just has too much opposition right now."

"Captain Callahan will take a minimum crew along on the tracking mission," Andrew figured. "They will actually act as the target because our ship is highly classified and is nearly impossible to detect."

"Remember the old F-117 Stealth Fighter that was first put into combat a long time ago?" said Cody. "I saw the specs on that, and they had to attach a small golf-ball sized pyramid of metal so that the airport radar could even track it! The detection equipment of that day wasn't very good. Today that fighter would stick out like a brass band in a hospital zone."

"It's a good thing that Mom designed our ship well," added Jennifer. "We're going to need all the stealth capacity possible to sneak into the quadrant where Dad and Mom disappeared."

"Come on, we'd better locate the Captain and get briefed on the station damage," said Andrew. "This is going to be an interesting chapter in my journal," he said to Jen and Cody as they walked along.

. . . I don't know why I'm so tired tonight—maybe it's 'cause Cody kept me up last night. If he doesn't stop having those nightmares . . . I don't know what Jen and I are going to do. He's wearing us out. I know what Mom would say about Cody. "Andrew, real love requires sacrifice!" I wonder what kind of sacrifices she was talking about? Surely she wasn't talking about sacrificing sleep for a nerdy little bro, was she?

Later,
Andrew

love suffers long
love never fails

love is kind
love thinks no evil
love does not envy

Sounds like somebody has some real wisdom—mainly Andrew's mom. She was right! Love is not just something you feel, but it is demonstrated through our sacrificial actions toward another. Real love does require the action of sacrifice. You might be asking: But what are these sacrificial actions? Take the example of Andrew and Jen. What did they give up to demonstrate love to Cody? They could have disregarded his nightmare or made fun of him. Instead, they gave up some sleep to comfort him and make him feel secure and loved. So, you might say, they sacrificed sleep to demonstrate love and concern.

Other ways to demonstrate love include things like sacrificing your personal time to help your parents, to assist neighbors who are in need, or to pray for friends who are not Christians or are having trouble. Giving up some of your allowance to help buy groceries for the homeless also requires a sacrifice of money. We can tell someone we love them, but being willing to sacrifice time, money or possessions really demonstrates love to others.

If you are ever tempted to complain about the small sacrifices God might be asking you to make as you demonstrate love to others, perhaps you should remember the Lord Jesus Christ. What was He willing to sacrifice for you? Think about it!

Cadet Challenge 5.1

1 Corinthians 13:1–3

Draw symbols in place of the missing words to make a rebus.

Though [ ] [ ] with the [ ] of [ ] and of [ ], but have not [ ], I have become sounding brass or a clanging [ ]. And though [ ] have the [ ] of prophecy, and [ ] all [ ] and all [ ], and though [ ] have all [ ], so that [ ] could remove [ ], but have not [ ], I am [ ]. And though [ ] bestow all my goods to [ ] the [ ], and though [ ] give my body to be [ ] but have not [ ], it profits me [ ].

Cadet Challenge 5.2

Love Is . . . and Love Is Not . . .

Read the passage below. Write what love is in the first column and what love is not in the second column. Then circle two areas in which your love needs to grow.

I Corinthians 13:4-8

v. 4 "Love suffers long and is kind; love does not envy; love does not parade itself, is not puffed up;

v. 5 does not behave rudely, does not seek its own, is not provoked, thinks no evil;

v. 6 does not rejoice in iniquity, but rejoices in the truth;

v. 7 bears all things, believes all things, hopes all things, endures all things.

v. 8a Love never fails . . . ."

	Love Is . . .	Love Is Not . . .
v. 4	kind	puffed up
v. 5	polite	provoked
v. 6	happy w truth	happy w sin
v. 7	hopeful	hopeless
v. 8a	never failing	going to fail

Meeting Needs

What needs do people have?

How did Jesus meet the needs of people?

What can we do to meet people's needs?

How does God meet my needs?

ANDREW

Dear Diary,

What a mess we have up here—another accident! It looks like a soup can exploded. I'm not sure exactly what's happened yet—Captain, Officer Bryant and Navigator James are assessing the need. All I know is—we are going to have to work hard to fix this one. It's gonna' take a miracle all right. I should go and help, but I'm kinda' tired of always getting interrupted in the middle of my writing. I don't know—maybe I'm just lazy or something.

"Wow! Look how that outer wheel bulkhead is peeled back. How will we ever get that repaired in time for our launch, Officer Bryant?" questioned Jennifer.

"It's going to take some real work, but the 'bots are already on the job fabricating hull plates and truss members," he replied. "Those tireless little workers keep us from having to go out there as often as the astronauts did in the early days."

"I suppose you want me to do EVAC work," said Andrew reluctantly.

"You've got it!" said Officer Bryant. "Remember that any time extra vehicular activity is called for, it is always dangerous. I know it's not something you actually look forward to doing."

"You can say that again," Andrew complained.

"I'd rather stay inside my quarters," Cody quietly commented under his breath.

"Com'on you guys." Jennifer encouraged. "The crew needs our help."

"There's the Captain now with Officer James. Looks like he has the duty roster," Officer Bryant said as he picked up the pace.

The crew gathered around Captain Callahan and waited for him to organize his notes.

"All right crew, this is the way it's going to be," he said very business-like. "We'll all work together to get this repair done on time so we don't lose our launch window. That means long duty hours, no trips down to planet and minimal recreational time. We have a job to do, and we're going to do it."

"Oh man, there goes my extra writing time," Andrew grumbled.

"What was that, Cadet?" the Captain said, interrupting himself.

"Nothing, sir," Andrew said cautiously. "I was just making a verbal note to myself, sir."

"Very well. Officer James, you will be lending your expertise to the team responsible for rewiring the NAV beacons. Take young Cody with you. I'd like him to become familiar with the operations side of your department."

"Yes, sir," Officer James responded.

"Officer Bryant will be assisted by Cadets Andrew and Jennifer. Your group will be assigned to the equipment relocation team to clear the hangar decks so the new wheel sections can be fitted and secured."

"That is all. I need Cadets Andrew, Jennifer and Cody in my office in three," the Captain added.

"Uh oh! I shouldn't have made that crack about my journal," Andrew whispered to Jennifer.

"Maybe it's about something else," Jennifer whispered back. "Come on, we've only got three minutes."

The Captain's back was turned to them as they entered quietly. He was standing by the portal and gazing off into the black velvet expanse. His hands were clasped behind his back, but not in a tense way. The three cadets stood by and quietly waited, knowing that he was aware of their presence.

"This accident hasn't been easy for any of us," he finally said, breaking the long silence. The Captain turned to face them. "I've got some good news and some not-so-good news," he said slowly, letting the words sink in as the Cadets held their breath.

Finally Cody couldn't help himself any longer and blurted out, "The mission is still on, isn't it, Captain Callahan?"

"Oh yes, the news isn't that bad," he replied quickly. "What I've learned from Command is that the station personnel need help. We have the knowledge and abilities to really lend assistance, but it would mean a delay in our departure by a month. Command is allowing us to make the final decision."

Captain Callahan continued, "Cody, the abilities you have to compute navigational plots is well known. If you are comfortable with the adjusted launch window, I say we stay and meet these needs here, but it's your call. We can be of tremendous assistance in their time of need if we can put our own plans on the back jets for awhile."

Andrew was feeling a bit embarrassed now about his off-hand remark, but the Captain didn't bring it up.

"As I see it, Captain Callahan, we should have no problem with our launch window," Cody concluded after a little reflection on the math computations. "The planets we are going to use for gravity assist give us a wide window this time of year. The station will need a miracle worker to do these repairs, and if we can help at all, I say it's okay with me."

"Andrew? Jennifer?" The Captain glanced at each of them.

"We're fine with that, Captain," Jennifer said. "It wouldn't be very professional to have the skills and tools that could help out in a crisis and then, when approached for assistance, to deny that help."

"Good, I was hoping you would see it that way." The Captain was obviously pleased—with the Cadet's decision anyway. "Let's help those who can't fully help themselves right now."

Jennifer locked arms with her brothers. They stood together for a moment gazing through the portal at God's creation.

"Okay, gang, we need to do what Captain says. We need to help those who can't help themselves," Jennifer said. "After all . . . haven't we all needed help at one time or another?"

"Uh huh . . ." Cody said, remembering how Jennifer especially had helped him when he was having those terrible nightmares.

"Well then," Jennifer said. "Let's go to work!"

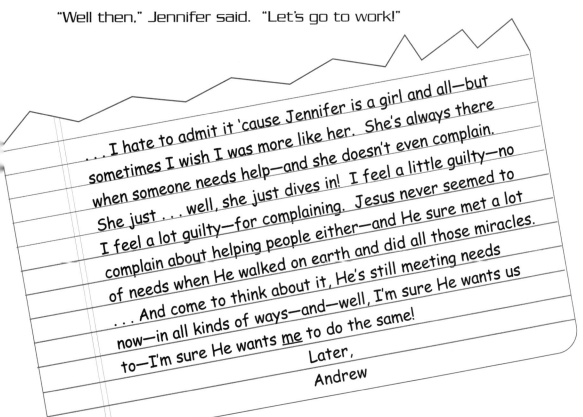

. . . I hate to admit it 'cause Jennifer is a girl and all—but sometimes I wish I was more like her. She's always there when someone needs help—and she doesn't even complain. She just . . . well, she just dives in! I feel a little guilty—no I feel a lot guilty—for complaining. Jesus never seemed to complain about helping people either—and He sure met a lot of needs when He walked on earth and did all those miracles. . . . And come to think about it, He's still meeting needs now—in all kinds of ways—and—well, I'm sure He wants us to—I'm sure He wants me to do the same!

Later,

Andrew

Andrew is right! Jennifer is a good example of a person who seems always ready to lend a hand to someone in need. And she does so without grumbling. God desires us to do the same.

You might be asking: What kinds of needs are we to meet? Are we just supposed to meet physical needs, or are there other needs God wants us to meet? Some of the ways the Bible says we are to meet those needs might surprise you. For example, not only does the Bible teach us to provide for people's physical needs, but God's Word exhorts us to serve Christ by meeting emotional and spiritual needs as well.

The Bible specifically gives us many "one-another" commands that tell us how to meet physical, emotional and spiritual needs. In Romans 15:7 God tells us to receive one another. But how does receiving one another meet a need? Think about it! How do you feel when you are warmly received into a group, onto a team or into a new class? Do you feel accepted and valued? When you receive other people, they feel accepted, too. In other words, when we receive someone, we have the potential of meeting that person's spiritual need or their emotional need for significance or security. Putting into practice God's "one-another" commands helps us to do that. This week think about how you can meet another person's physical, emotional or spiritual needs.

Cadet Challenge 6.1

Use a dictionary to write a brief definition or synonym for each underlined word in the verse. Then in your own words, paraphrase the meaning of the verse in the space below.

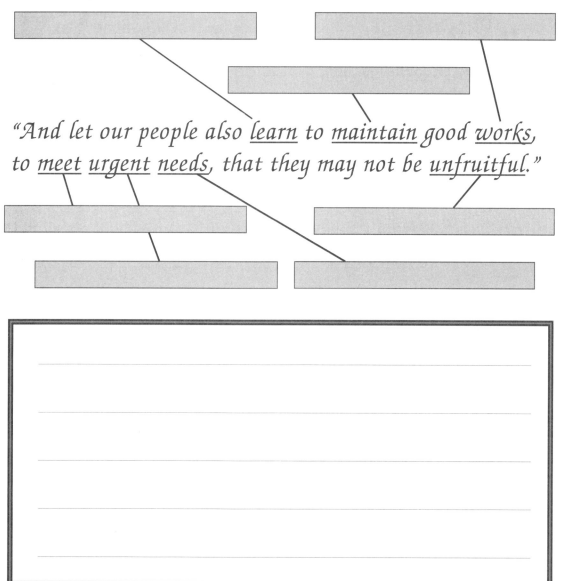

"And let our people also learn to maintain good works, to meet urgent needs, that they may not be unfruitful."

Cadet Challenge 6.2

What Are the "One-Another" Commands?

Look up the verses and write the "one-another" commands using only a few words.

1. Romans 15:7 _____

2. Romans 16:16a _____

3. Galatians 6:2 _____

4. Colossians 3:16 _____

5. James 5:16 _____

6. I Corinthians 12:24–25 _____

7. Ephesians 4:31–32 (I) _____

8. Ephesians 4:31–32 (2) _____

9. Galatians 5:13–14 _____

10. Ephesians 4:1–3 _____

Knowing Jesus Christ

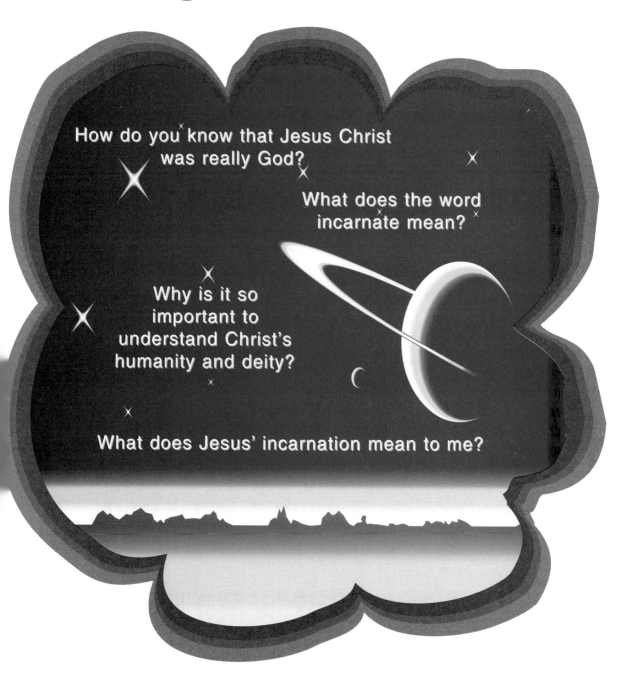

How do you know that Jesus Christ was really God?

What does the word incarnate mean?

Why is it so important to understand Christ's humanity and deity?

What does Jesus' incarnation mean to me?

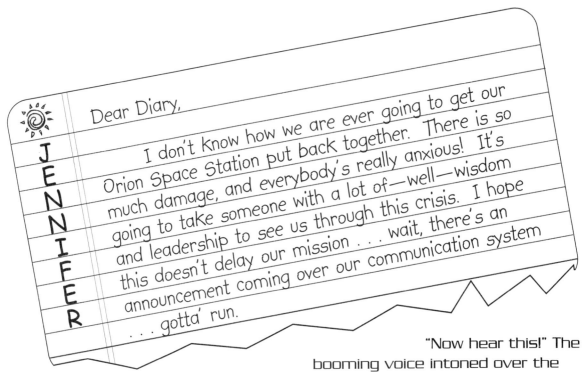

Dear Diary,

I don't know how we are ever going to get our Orion Space Station put back together. There is so much damage, and everybody's really anxious! It's going to take someone with a lot of—well—wisdom and leadership to see us through this crisis. I hope this doesn't delay our mission . . . wait, there's an announcement coming over our communication system . . . gotta' run.

J
E
N
N
I
F
E
R

"Now hear this!" The booming voice intoned over the entire orbiting space station Orion, echoing from curved wall to curved wall. "This is Fleet Admiral Haynes. All repair crew, report to the staging area near Alpha Quadrant. Those cleared for EVAC duty have priority in the tube transports."

"Wow," exclaimed Andrew, "the Port Admiral himself is taking direct command of the operation!"

"Wow, is right," commented Officer Bryant. "I've never even seen an Admiral, so this must really be top priority for him to be directly involved."

"Top priority and then some," agreed Andrew as they loped along the tubes toward Alpha. They jumped off the rail transports to take a shortcut on foot. "It's not often that a space station the size of Orion has an entire section of its outer wheel blown into space. Thank the Lord that it was a cargo section and there was no loss of life."

Officer Bryant glanced at his wrist computer. "Okay, Andrew, my locator says we are nearing the meeting point. Watch for the exit tube on the left."

Elsewhere, Officer James and Cody were assisting the electronics and navigation teams reprogramming the beacons. Cody was doing such a good job that Officer James was actually beginning to admire him.

"I'm impressed," Officer James reluctantly admitted. "Maybe you're not such a bad partner after all."

"Oh, it's nothing," said Cody. "Captain Callahan made me do special exercises when I kept beating the simulators at the Academy."

Officer James was stunned! He'd never beaten the simulator even once, and he was tops in his class at the Academy.

"All EVAC personnel, meet me in the Alpha staging area on Deck C," boomed the intercom. The Admiral seemed to be speaking right inside their minds as both headphones were activated in their space suits.

"Just imagine," wondered Jennifer as she and Captain Callahan caught up with the rest of his crew. "We're going to actually see the Admiral! We've only heard about him for years, how distinguished he is—almost unapproachable. Now he's right here on this station."

"Kind of makes you wonder if he's even real," said Andrew through his helmet faceplate. He hadn't been sealed in yet, so the visor was up.

"Let me tell you something, Cadets," Captain Callahan said quietly. "You have been training for a mission that the Admiral is personally interested in. Your minds are filled with facts and skills no one else could have mastered. He has high expectations for how you will perform and hopes to present you to the Federation Council as a success story for the Academy. You've learned to "talk the talk" so now let's "walk the walk"!

"Oh, Captain," said Jennifer. "We'd do anything to please the Admiral!"

Officers James and Bryant nodded together as one. "You know we're behind this mission with all jets blasting full, Captain."

Just then the crowded hangar deck seemed to represent an ocean with a giant whale swimming just under the surface as the crowds parted in waves to let someone pass—someone having so much authority that the crowds gave way without so much as a spoken command by the security officers.

It was the Admiral himself! He took long strides, staring straight ahead as though on a mission. The security officers could barely keep up. He walked briskly and headed straight for the three cadets.

"Captain Callahan, introduce me to your crew!" The Admiral's voice was even more commanding in person. It was probably because he was a head taller than everyone around him.

"Admiral Haynes, my First Officer Bryant, Navigator James and of course you remember Cadets Andrew, Jennifer and Cody." Captain Callahan made the last a statement rather than a question.

The deck was spellbound! Here was the Admiral. In the past, he was only a voice over the COM or a scrawled signature on an order. Now he had actually come down from central command in the hub and interacted with them in person, showing he really cared about each of them.

To the Cadets alone the Admiral confided something only the Captain knew and had kept secret all this time. "Cadets," he began, "I haven't told this to anyone here except your Captain. You are very special to me. Your mother was my only daughter. That makes me your . . . your grandfather."

Andrew, Jennifer and Cody were speechless! The Admiral, the Commander of the most powerful Federation in the known universe, was their grandfather! That meant that they were related to him.

"I know you are very special children," the Admiral continued softly. "God has blessed each of you with special gifts, and your mother and father nurtured you for whatever job the Lord has chosen for you. Perhaps this mission is your calling. Please bring my daughter and her husband back to us all. The full resources of the Federation and every power at my command will be behind you all the way. The Lord be with you all!"

Turning back to Orion's crew, the Admiral continued. "This mission depends on each of you giving yourself completely to the cause. I know you will be successful." The hangar deck cheered the encouraging challenges the Admiral made regarding the necessary repairs. The three Cadets heard nothing but the Admiral's last words resounding in their minds— ". . . your grandfather . . . the full resources of the Federation and every power at my command behind you all the way."

What kind of a mission was this going to be anyway?

What a day—what a day! We're still speechless. The rest of the crew still can't believe it either—they can't believe that the top chief—Admiral Haynes himself—would think enough of us to take direct command of the repair operation—and that he came and showed his personal interest in our wellbeing. Can you imagine Admiral Haynes coming to the Orion Space Station? And then . . . wow . . . he told Cody, Andrew and me that he was our grandfather. Our grandfather—imagine that! We are actually related to Admiral Haynes, the commander of the most powerful federation in the Known universe . . . Wow, again!

Jen

Just as Admiral Haynes came from Central Command just in time to help, so it was when Jesus Christ came to rescue sinners. Have you ever thought about how the God of the universe became a Man? Why would our omniscient and powerful God want to become a Man? Well, if He hadn't, we would be in big trouble. God's Son needed to become a Man to be a suitable sacrifice for man's sin. It took a perfect Man to die for sinful men. That perfect Man was Jesus!

Have you trusted in the death and resurrection of God's perfect Son, Jesus Christ, to save you? Have you trusted Him as your personal perfect substitute? If you have, then you are related to God as one of His children. Think about it! Just as Andrew, Jen and Cody are related to Admiral Haynes, a most powerful commander, so you are related to the most powerful Person in the universe, the God-Man, Jesus Christ.

Your Bible lessons will focus on an event called the incarnation. The incarnation of Jesus Christ was when God became a man. Jesus took on a human form while remaining sinless in order to rescue us and keep us from being separated from Him for eternity. This week ask yourself, "What does incarnation mean to me?"

Cadet Challenge 7.1

John 1:14

Write the letters, along with the words and phrases, in the order they appear in the passage.

A	and we	_____	_____
B	the glory	_____	_____
C	and dwelt	_____	_____
D	the Word	_____	_____
E	as of	_____	_____
F	His glory	_____	_____
G	the only	_____	_____
H	And	_____	_____
I	beheld	_____	_____
J	full of	_____	_____
K	became flesh	_____	_____
L	among us	_____	_____
M	begotten of	_____	_____
N	the Father	_____	_____
O	truth	_____	_____
P	grace and	_____	_____

Cadet Challenge 7.2

═══ Was Jesus a Man or Was He God? ═══

Read the verses and decide which ones show Jesus as a man and which show Him as God. In the appropriate column, write several words that explain your reason.

References	MAN	GOD
1. Matthew 4:2		
2. John 10:30–33		
3. John 1:1		
4. John 4:6		
5. John 14:8–9		
6. Philippians 2:5–6		
7. John 11:35		
8. Hebrews 4:15		
9. Colossians 2:9		
10. I Timothy 2:5		
11. Titus 2:13		

Choosing Wisdom

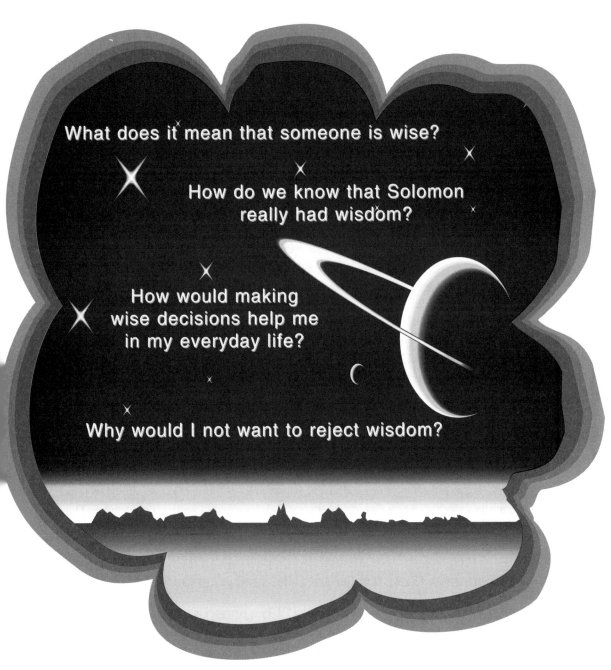

What does it mean that someone is wise?

How do we know that Solomon really had wisdom?

How would making wise decisions help me in my everyday life?

Why would I not want to reject wisdom?

Dear Diary,

All of us cadets are still trying to get over the Admiral coming down to help us. Thanks to him we are ready to go on with the final tests . . . uhhh . . . Speaking of final tests . . . I think I might need to go and help.

— JENNIFER

"Captain Callahan, Officer James here, sir. We've wrapped up this section and are ready to proceed to the final tests by linking with the main navigational computers at the hub."

"What! Already?" exclaimed the Captain incredulously. "I can't believe you did all that in only a week. Oh, wait a minute . . . you were working with Cadet Cody. That explains it. Great work, Officer James. Commendations are definitely in order," he added enthusiastically.

Officer James glowed with pride, although he knew the Captain was giving the Navigator credit for what was mostly Cody's success. He was amazed again as he thought about Cody's ability to solve problems and look ahead. Cody was young—but so good at discerning the real problem—so good at knowing what to do. He remembered once asking the Captain how Cody could be so smart. The Captain had replied, "At the Academy, Cody respected the higher-ups, simply asked them to teach him—and they did."

"Great news, Cody, the Captain was really pumped!" said Officer James.

"Anything to please the boss," Cody responded. "It's just like you said, Officer James. It is one thing to know all this stuff, but another thing entirely to apply it and make things work. I know lots of facts, but your practical experience is what really came through, Navigator."

"I guess we make a pretty good team after all," Officer James admitted.

From one of the transfer tube airlocks Andrew whistled. "Now that's something I never thought I'd hear. Cody must be growing up."

"Yeah," added Jennifer, bounding in right behind him. "That Cody—Mr. Walking Encyclopedia—is human after all."

"Actually, what Officer James and Cadet Cody probably meant was that real wisdom is learning to consistently apply the facts so as to benefit others as well as yourself," Officer Bryant interjected. "The wisest man who ever lived was faced with the same situation. God offered young King Solomon anything he desired (like money or power), but Solomon just asked for the wisdom to properly guide God's people. Because of that choice God gave him all the other things as well. He realized that real wisdom came from reverencing the Lord and understanding life from God's viewpoint."

"That's right, Officer Bryant," agreed Jennifer. "For example, if all Andrew did was just watch ships take off and orbit, he'd never be one of the best pilots around. Just look how we've all been able to help repair Station Orion by putting our knowledge to work." Jennifer was beaming. She was so proud of her brothers and what the whole team had accomplished that week.

Captain Callahan now joined in with his own observation. "I am really proud of all of you and so is Admiral Haynes," the Captain said. "We could have just told the station personnel that this explosion on Alpha Deck was their problem and then gone ahead with our mission. It's far better to sympathize with how others are feeling and then do something about it rather than to just say, 'Oh, that's too bad' and then walk away."

"Now hear this," the COM startled them all back to the job at hand. It was Admiral Haynes' commanding voice. "I want all station personnel to muster in the Observation Hall for final re-pressurization instructions. EVAC teams are to re-deploy afterward and position themselves at all bulkhead sections to check for leaks."

After everyone had assembled, the Admiral continued, "All team leaders and their crews are to be highly commended for an outstanding job. Simply outstanding! You accomplished in one week what could have taken a month to finish even under the best of circumstances. My congratulations for the successful application of the skills you developed during your years at the Academy. You've all earned planet-side liberty starting with the next cargo supply ship arriving from Siberia."

"Now let's re-pressurize and prove our work!" the Admiral challenged with his closing words.

Andrew and Officer Bryant dashed off to the transport shuttle to suit up for their last EVAC duty.

"Working weightless in space is much harder than in gravity on earth," explained Captain Callahan to the Cadets. "It takes effort to start an object moving since everything has mass. Yes, it's weightless, but one still has to get it moving first. Then you have to use as much effort to stop a motion as you used to start it moving in the first place, because now it has inertia, which is the tendency of a body to remain at rest or to stay in motion. EVAC work is constant and very tiring."

"Oh, I hope Andrew and Officer Bryant are well rested for the job," said Jennifer, concerned.

"They'll be fine, I'm sure," the Captain added. "But it will be a lot of work. Once objects start moving, they keep moving in space. There is almost no air resistance or drag in a low Earth orbit. There is some, however."

"Isn't that what brought America's first space station down?" asked Jennifer.

"Good memory, Jen!" exclaimed the Captain. "Skylab was to be in orbit much longer, but increased sunspot activity heated the upper atmosphere. The atmosphere expanded further out into space—

enough to allow a few air molecules to crash into the station. But that little bit slowed down its orbital speed enough so that the gravitational attraction of Earth wasn't balanced by the centrifugal force of orbit."

"You know what happened next? It burned up over Australia and a piece of it actually landed on a beach. It was found by a young boy who won the contest to search for pieces. The original space shuttle had engine design problems and wasn't finished in time to boost the station out of the atmosphere into a higher orbit," Officer James added.

"Another factor making space work difficult is the psychological burden of not letting anything get away from you. Even a little bolt or fastener can become a damaging, even deadly projectile if it drifts into the path of another satellite or spacecraft moving at a different orbital speed," the Captain explained.

"Wow, there is sure more to it than I initially thought," Andrew confessed. "I just realized I almost pulled the wrong lever earlier, and we might have become the second Skylab."

"Uhuh! I guess . . . every move has to be considered carefully before acting. Wouldn't it be great if we were . . . well . . . as wise with all our behavior?" Jennifer said, poking fun at Andrew.

Boy! Andrew's statement scared me a little. We could have been the second space station to leave pieces along the shores of Australia. That's how it must be when we are using wisdom. You use wisdom, and you're okay. You lose wisdom, and you're . . . well . . . not okay. Did I just write a poem or something?

Jennifer

71

Jennifer might not have written a real honest-to-goodness poem, but what she said was nevertheless right. When you use wisdom, you are okay. But when you lose wisdom, you're not okay. It's a simple statement, but it is absolutely true.

King Solomon in the Old Testament knew how important it was to have wisdom, especially in spiritual matters. In 1 Kings 3:9 he asked God for wisdom and then asked a very insightful question. "Therefore give to Your servant an understanding heart to judge Your people, that I may discern between good and evil. For who is able to judge this great people of Yours?" In other words, it is impossible for any human being, given his or her imperfections, to know how to judge anything right or wrong. People can only judge good and evil when God has given them an understanding mind and heart—or wisdom. That is why it is so important to have wisdom.

Check the questions you would most like to answer this week.

☐ Would you like to know for sure that you are making wise choices—all the time?

☐ Would you feel secure if you were giving good advice to your friends 100% percent of the time?

☐ Is it important for you to understand what God wants you to do every day?

☐ Would you like to avoid the hard consequences of living life without wisdom?

Get on board — let's find out about wisdom!
Get on board — let's find out about wisdom!
Get on board — let's find out about wisdom!

Cadet Challenge 8.1

Draw a Rebus

Look up the verses and draw symbols to complete Proverbs 2:1–5.

"My [____], if [____] receive my [____],

and [____] my commands within you, so

that [____] incline your [____] to [____],

and apply your [____] to understanding; yes, if

you [____] out [____] discernment, and lift

your [____] for understanding, if you [____] up

her as [____], and search [____] her as for

hidden [____], then you [____] understand

the [____] of the Lord and [____] the

knowledge of [____]."

Cadet Challenge 8.2

1 Kings 3:5–15

	Who?	What?	When?	Where?	Why?
Verse 5					
Verse 6					
Verses 7-9					
Verses 10-14					
Verse 15					

Determining to Do Right

What happens to people who determine to do right?

What characteristics are needed to stand alone?

Would God ever ask me to stand alone if I were in danger?

How does God help me do the right thing?

Dear Diary,

I wish you could talk, Diary, because sometimes I just don't know what to do. You see—I'm getting pressure from some of the new crewmembers. The other day one of them tried to get me to listen to—well—this joke. I could tell it was going the wrong way. Then another crewmember began laughing his head off. I tried not to laugh, but I felt—well—a little stupid. What am I supposed to do? I want to tell Jennifer . . . but—well—she would probably give me a lecture or something. Speaking of Jennifer . . . she's trying to get my attention now. I'll write later.

"Cody, can we talk?" Jennifer asked.

"Oh . . . uhh . . . sure," Cody said.

"Cody, what's the matter? You've really been quiet lately," Jennifer said, showing real concern toward her brother. She'd always known her little brother to be cheerful most of the time. True, he was a bit timid and sometimes scared over the dumbest things, but his current mood just wasn't normal.

"Oh, it's probably nothing," Cody mumbled. "It's just that—well—it's just . . . ."

"Just what, Cody? You can tell me," Jen said.

"Well, it's just—some of the things the crew tried to get me to do during the week we were working on the navigation equipment. Not Officer James or Navigator Bryant—but some of the new crew."

"What happened?" Jennifer asked, feeling concerned now.

"Well, promise not to tell the Captain?"

"You know we can't promise that sort of thing if laws or rules are being broken, Cody." Jennifer was being a Senior Cadet now and not a big sister.

"It's nothing like that, Sis—it's just that some of the crew were trying to get me to do things that I knew weren't right for someone my age—like drinking stuff or telling dirty jokes to make people laugh."

"Remember what Mom said before we went off to the Academy?" Jennifer reminded him. "She said we'd face all kinds of things that would not be helpful in our lives. Most cadets would be busy studying to reach their goals; others would be more interested in sharing a good time and would drop out early. She knew we would come face to face with some of life's choices."

"Yeah, I remember. She said we should determine before we even go out of our home exactly what our boundaries would be. Also, we should expect to be tested by our friends—and prepare a wise response to their dares. They might not have the same boundaries as we do."

Cody thought for a moment. "You know, Jen? I guess it actually worked just like Mom said it would. I just made a joke about why I wouldn't go partying with them—and everyone laughed and left me alone—well—after they tried to talk me into it a few more times."

"She knew it would, Cody. It's the same with Andrew and me when we've kept people from talking us into doing something that would be displeasing to the Lord. You've got to have a game plan before someone throws you the ball—so to speak," Jennifer added.

"But they laughed at me—and—well—I wanted to belong," he moaned. "I've always been different from everybody."

"Well—join the club, Cody. We're all different. Mom and Dad knew that when we were just babies." Jennifer was firm with him, hoping to shake him out of his mood.

"You know what to do, so just do it," she encouraged. "The Lord will give you the grace and a way out. Just don't get into a situation where you get backed into a corner and lose control."

"Thanks, Sis, I really needed to get that off my mind. I know the crew means well, but sometimes they don't seem to have any convictions. They would rather have fun than to do right," said Cody, jumping off the bulkhead cot as it flipped back up into the stowed position. "Come on, let's go help Andrew get out of his EVAC suit and see what adventures he'll add to his journal."

Meanwhile, outside the space station Orion, Officer Bryant and Cadet Andrew were scanning each bulkhead seam with special electronic gas detectors, making sure each connection was absolutely airtight.

"It's the slow, small leaks that can be the most deadly," crackled Andrew's helmet speakers as Officer Bryant came up over the far side of the last major section seal. Their EVAC suits protected them from the frigid cold of space. "I want to finish this in time for the crew party celebrating the completion of the repairs," Officer Bryant added.

"Yeah, I want to go, too. It should really be fun with everyone there," Andrew replied.

"Hold it, I'm getting a reading here. Finish scanning the seam up to me, and then let's use your detector and compare readings. This doesn't look good," Officer Bryant observed.

"What about the party, Officer Bryant? We'll miss everything if we don't finish in another hour!" Andrew was sounding disappointed now.

"Forget parties, Cadet Andrew, we have a job to do and people are depending on us to do it right the first time."

Officer Bryant shifted into teaching mode. "We can't put our personal desires ahead of the crew's trust in us. There will be lots of time for fun and games during your career. Right now, we're supposed to be assuring the integrity of the gas seals on the hull. Every single molecule of air is far more precious than gold up here in space, and we're going to make sure they all stay confined to the station.

Andrew joined Officer Bryant and set about reseating the fasteners and adding the extra sealant to that area. Once the material had set, they checked for leaks again and found none.

"Now we can sleep tonight, knowing that our air will not be lost to space," said Officer Bryant. "You know we made the right decision, Andrew, to continue on with this job until it was really done."

"Yeah, I know, sir," Andrew agreed. "There wasn't really any question about it. I sure feel a lot better about doing what I know to be right than I would if I had only done half a job."

Together they pulsed their suit jets guiding the EVAC units toward the airlock. Andrew took one last look at the bright blue ball of Earth down below. The slow rotation of the station's wheels and spokes made the whole scene look like some kind of graceful dance in the heavens.

"I wonder if there will be any cake and punch left," he thought to himself.

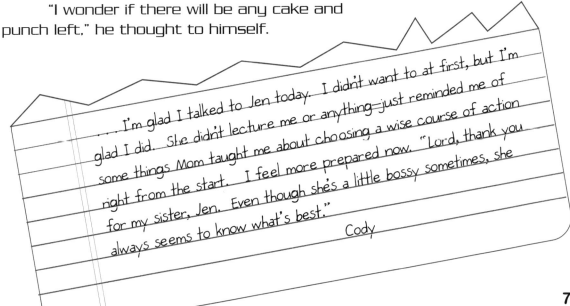

...I'm glad I talked to Jen today. I didn't want to at first, but I'm glad I did. She didn't lecture me or anything—just reminded me of some things Mom taught me about choosing a wise course of action right from the start. I feel more prepared now. "Lord, thank you for my sister, Jen. Even though she's a little bossy sometimes, she always seems to know what's best."

Cody

Have you ever been in a dilemma like Cody? Are you ever tempted to do something that you know is wrong? Have your friends told you things like, "It's okay to laugh at a little dirty joke once in a while." Or, "I can look at your answers on the test just this one time." Or, "You can lie to your parents just one time and then never do it again." Perhaps you have some friends in your classroom, neighborhood or even church who are like Cody's crewmembers. Maybe you have cousins who are not the best influence on you. How do you handle this kind of peer pressure? How do you stand for what you know is right when your friends and relatives seem to be doing what is wrong? Well, hang on—because there is someone who lived over 2,500 years ago who had similar problems.

God's prophet Daniel lived in hard times. He and his friends had been captured and taken to live in a pagan country under ungodly rule. God had given instructions to His people. One instruction was that God's people were not to eat meat offered to idols. Since most of the young men in Daniel's community saw nothing wrong with eating meat offered to idols, Daniel and his three friends had two choices. They could avoid the peer pressure by disobeying God and eating the meat, or they could obey God by standing for what they believed even though it meant being ridiculed by friends. What did they do? That is just one of the many questions we will answer this week as we discuss ways we can be more consistent in determining to do right.

Cadet Challenge 9.1

Write the verses in the four different versions below. Answer the questions on the next page, then write your own paraphrase.

New King James Version

King James Version

New International Version

New American Standard Bible

Cadet Challenge 9.1 continued

Psalm 1:1−2

Compare:

1. Which version begins with a sentence ending with an exclamation mark?

_____

2. In which versions is a synonym used for the word "path"?

_____

3. What is the other word?

_____

4. In which version is "mockers" used?

_____

5. What synonyms are used for "mockers," and in what versions?

_____

6. What synonym for "ungodly" is used, and in what versions?

_____

Write Your Paraphrase

_____

_____

_____

_____

_____

Cadet Challenge 9.2

═══════Who Determined . . . to Do Right? ═══════

Answer the questions according to Daniel 1:1–21.

1. When did the story take place? _____

_____

2. Which king defeated whom? Who was taken captive?

_____

3. Nebuchadnezzar was king of which country? _____

_____

4. Who was the master of the king's eunuchs (servants)?

_____

5. What were the qualities the king had instructed Ashpenaz to find
   in the young men? _____

_____

6. What were the young men's daily provision of food and drink?

_____

7. How long were the young men supposed to train?

_____

Cadet Challenge 9.2 continued

8. What did the king want the young men to do after they were trained? _____

   _____

9. What names did the eunuch give to the four men?

   _____

10. Who would not defile himself with the king's food? Write out the verse with the reference. _____

    _____

11. Why was the eunuch worried? _____

    _____

12. What was the test that Daniel suggested? _____

    _____

13. What was the result of the test? _____

    _____

14. What did God give the young men? Why do you think God blessed them? _____

    _____

15. How did the king find the young men in matters of wisdom?

    _____

Worshiping God

What is the first step to worship?

Who does God seek to worship Him?

What is the meaning of worshiping God in spirit and truth?

How can I improve my worship?

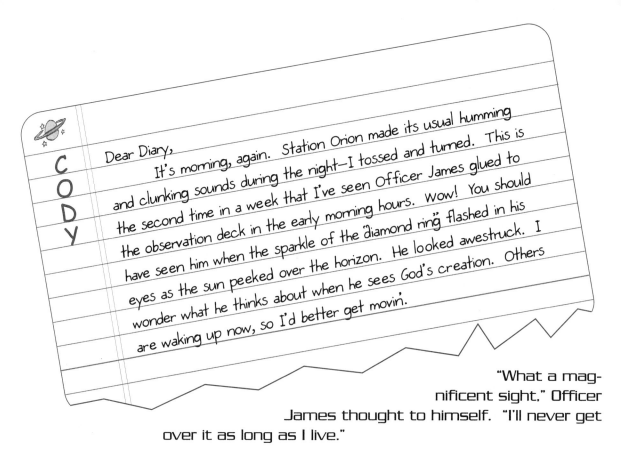

Dear Diary,
It's morning, again. Station Orion made its usual humming and clunking sounds during the night—I tossed and turned. This is the second time in a week that I've seen Officer James glued to the observation deck in the early morning hours. Wow! You should have seen him when the sparkle of the "diamond ring" flashed in his eyes as the sun peeked over the horizon. He looked awestruck. I wonder what he thinks about when he sees God's creation. Others are waking up now, so I'd better get movin'.

"What a magnificent sight," Officer James thought to himself. "I'll never get over it as long as I live."

Officer James was not known among the crew for emotional comments. In fact, most thought of him as a walking computer, all business-like and no fun.

It was Sunday. Chapel services were about to begin. Officer James never saw much purpose in chapel. "Too many religions, and they all think they are the only way to Heaven." he usually commented when someone asked him to attend a particular church.

"Rats! I told you we were going to miss it, Jennifer. You and your hair!" Cody mumbled in frustration.

"Oh, hi, Officer James. I didn't see you there," said Cody, changing his tone of voice quickly.

"Good morning, Cody. Good morning, Jennifer and Andrew," Officer James said, greeting the others as they came around the bulkhead into the observation area. "What brings you over this way so early? You're quartered near Alpha Deck close to your ship."

"Oh, we were hoping to see the sunrise on our way to chapel, but some people want to have their hair just right before they go out in public," Cody verbally jabbed at Jennifer again.

"Stop it, Cody. I just want to look my best for the day. It is Sunday, you know," she countered.

Andrew jumped in, "She'll be fine soon, sir. It's just that she is having one of those unmanageable 'bad hair days' I keep hearing about," he teased.

"Stop it!" Jennifer exclaimed.

"Well, you of all people, Jen, should know that the Lord looks on the heart and not on the external things when you worship Him," Andrew said more seriously.

"Officer James, would you join us for Sunday worship? We're on our way right now," Andrew offered.

"Thanks, but maybe some other time, Cadets. I'll just stay here and do my own thing if you don't mind. I can't see how going to a service makes any difference, anyway. Everybody seems to prefer a different church or form of worship— and they can't all be right, can they?"

"Many of them may not be right, sir." Andrew was being careful here. "You see, the Lord isn't so concerned about the brand of church or whether or not you sing choruses or hymns, but rather that you are worshiping Him with your whole heart, in your innermost being. Looks like you were worshiping Him through His creation as you watched the sunrise, Officer James. You were blessed by its beauty, right?"

"I wouldn't say I was 'worshiping'—I was just . . . admiring the view," Officer James corrected.

"That's a little bit like worship in that you were admiring God's creation—but not quite the same. When a person truly worships God, he responds to the things God has made—in his head by acknowledging the God who made all things—but also in his heart or spirit by believing in Him," Andrew said respectfully.

"You know, sir," Cody piped in. "I'd rather not be alone. The Bible says not to forsake the gathering of ourselves together in worship. We can become stronger as a group—really support each other when things get tough. Others may have already gone through the same struggles that we might be facing. We can gain insight through their experiences."

The group started slowly walking along together. Andrew and Jennifer were doing some of the talking, but Cody was the one who seemed to be getting Officer James' attention. Maybe the officer didn't feel as threatened by him.

"Then, what's the bottom line, Cody?" Officer James pressed. "I mean, if the externals are just differences in comfort zones, what is the crucial core of the matter?"

"Well, to *worship* God in your heart, you need to *have* Him in your heart. Jesus gave the answer to a teacher of the Jews who once asked the same question. What Jesus told him was that he had to be born again. Not physically—since that only brings you into the world—but spiritually so you can enter God's spiritual family." Cody stopped walking now and faced Officer James.

"You know, sir," he continued, "you are such a capable officer that you've probably never really felt you needed the Lord. Everything just keeps going your way—and we all know you work very hard. But the Lord is looking into your heart, and He sees that you're not willing to trust Him with your soul yet. When you do, His Spirit will become part of you. Then you'll actually be related to the Lord, born again into His family like all of us have been. That's the bottom line, sir!"

"Wow, that's some heavy stuff to think about, Cody." Officer James responded thoughtfully. "Maybe I will join you for the morning. I've got some things to clear up in my mind. If your Lord can create such a vast universe with such incredible beauty and power, I'm sure He will be patient with me a little longer."

. . . The chapel service was just great this morning. My heart was really dancing. I kept thinking about our conversation with Officer James. I really like Officer James—a lot. But he can't really worship God in his heart until—well—until he is born again. I want him to experience God's love in the way my parents do—or did before they . . . well, at least like Andrew and Jen and I do now. I want him to be able to worship God both in spirit and in truth.

Later,

Cody

What does it mean to worship the Lord in spirit and in truth? Or maybe you haven't thought about it much.

Andrew tried to explain it to Officer James. He described worshiping the Lord in spirit and truth as being twofold: acknowledging in your head that God is the Creator (truth), while at the same time believing in Him in your innermost being or heart (spirit).

Some people are hindered from worshiping in spirit and truth. Cody pointed to the problem in the story. Can you find the paragraph that gives one explanation of why people do not worship God in spirit and truth?

Cadet Challenge 10.1

John 4:23-24

Fill in the blanks with nouns and pronouns.

"But the _____ is coming, and now is,

when the true _____ will worship

the _____ in _____ and

_____; for the _____ is seeking

such to worship _____.   _____ is

_____, and _____ who worship

_____ must worship in _____

and _____."

Cadet Challenge 10.2

What Happened When?

Read John 4:1–30 and write a few sentences to summarize what happened in each of the sections.

John 4:1-6

_____

_____

John 4:7-10

_____

_____

John 4:11-14

_____

_____

John 4:15-20

_____

_____

John 4:21-24

_____

_____

John 4:25-30

_____

_____

Controlling Our Speech

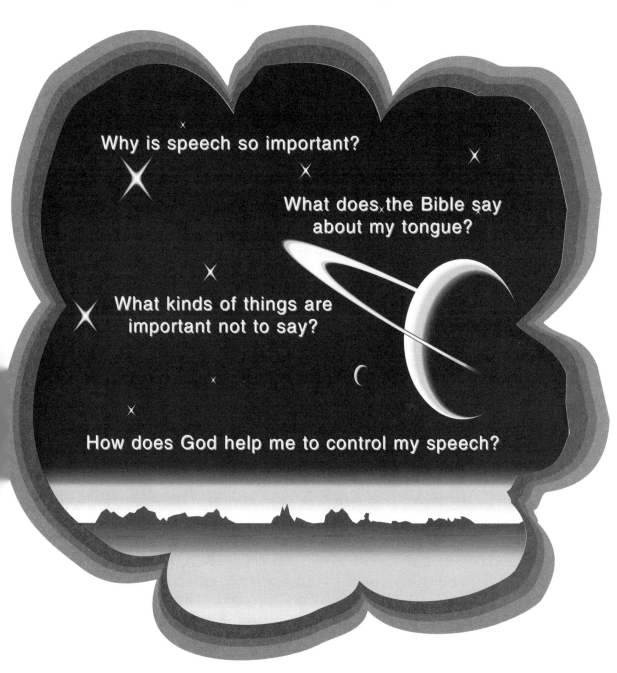

Why is speech so important?

What does the Bible say about my tongue?

What kinds of things are important not to say?

How does God help me to control my speech?

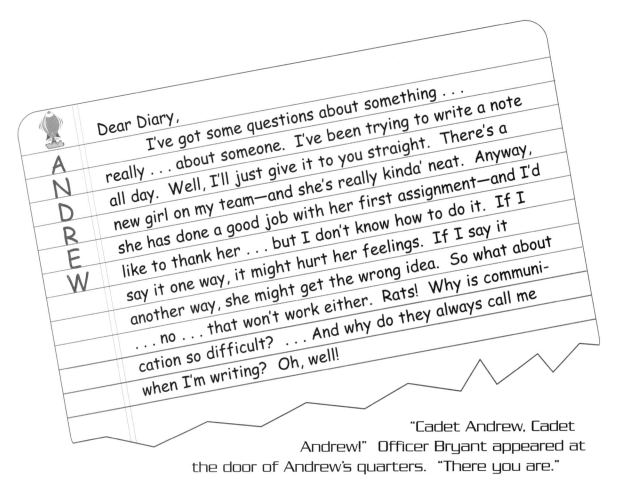

Dear Diary,

I've got some questions about something . . . really . . . about someone. I've been trying to write a note all day. Well, I'll just give it to you straight. There's a new girl on my team—and she's really kinda' neat. Anyway, she has done a good job with her first assignment—and I'd like to thank her . . . but I don't know how to do it. If I say it one way, it might hurt her feelings. If I say it another way, she might get the wrong idea. So what about . . . no . . . that won't work either. Rats! Why is communication so difficult? . . . And why do they always call me when I'm writing? Oh, well!

"Cadet Andrew, Cadet Andrew!" Officer Bryant appeared at the door of Andrew's quarters. "There you are."

"Yes sir?" Andrew said, looking up and trying not to act sheepish.

"I've been calling for you for a while now. At 30 past the hour the Captain has called for a meeting in . . . hey, what's the problem, Cadet?" Officer Bryant asked.

"Oh . . . oh . . . I'm fine, sir." Andrew said trying to shield his diary with his hand. "Well . . . sorta' fine. You see, the new girl that was assigned to my group helped us suit up for our EVAC work . . . and I was impressed with the way she did her job on those bulky space-suits, and yet at the same time . . . she was REALLY nice to us. Well sir, I just wanted to thank her—but I don't want to say the wrong thing. Like, I might sound like a dork, or something. I just want to be careful to get across exactly what I mean." Andrew looked up at the officer, who was now reading over his shoulder.

"That's very commendable, Andrew. Many people don't take the time to think about what they say or write, and the words might be inappropriate for that occasion. Why don't you just tell her what you think?"

"I can't do that, sir. I . . . I don't even know her last name yet. You were there—you saw her, remember?" Andrew pressed the question.

"Sounds to me like you are interested in this young lady," Bryant gently teased.

Andrew blushed. "Not really, sir."

"Well, that's fine," Officer Bryant said, getting serious again. "It's good to know the person next to you. After all, they may have your life in their hands as they work. Look, why don't you talk this over with Jennifer? I know Jen is your sister, but she'd know best of all how a young lady would react."

"Okay, sir. Maybe I'll ask Jen to give me a few point-ers," Andrew agreed.

"Don't forget the meeting at half past," Officer Bryant said.

Andrew waited until the officer had slipped out of sight, then he keyed in Jennifer's code and beeped her. "Hey, Sis, would you have time to help me with a communica-tion protocol? I want to make sure I say the right thing," he added, trying to act as if he were tending to business.

"Sure, but your journal doesn't need protocol—you just write down your impressions," said Jennifer, answering the page.

"Well, it's not exactly for my journal—I've already finished today's notes. It's for some . . . someone else," he confessed.

"Oh, really now," she commented slowly, drawing it out and teasing. "I think I'd better come right over."

Before Andrew walked from the communications console back to his desk, there was a knock at his door. It was Jennifer—already. She was panting a bit from rushing right over.

"Wow, that was faster than the shuttle in the EVAC tubes!" he exclaimed, somewhat startled. "You didn't have to come that quickly; it's just a simple question."

"Didn't sound 'simple' to me. Sounded like you're breaking new ground, and initial contact with 'alien species' must be handled very carefully. What if you said the wrong thing and she bit off your head?" she said, suppressing the urge to smile.

"How did you know she was a she?" he said surprised.

"Aha! You just told me," she giggled. "I could tell from the way you asked that you were somewhat embarrassed to approach me. I was wondering how long it would take you to meet someone that you liked."

"I don't like her—I just want to thank her. Good grief, does everything have to be a marriage proposal?" Andrew countered defensively.

"Don't be so sensitive, big brother. I'm on your side—and I'm here to help. You called me, remember?" Jennifer said.

Jennifer always seemed logical to Andrew. Even though she was younger that he was, she had a calming effect on him.

"You've heard some of the crew talking about other crew members, right? It has not always been uplifting or even polite conversation, has it?" she asked. "Words can have a tremendous effect on someone's feelings. They can also influence someone's impression of another person even before they meet."

"I know all that, Jen—so how can I say what I want to say and not give wrong impressions to others?" Andrew asked.

"Why don't you pray about what you should say—and how you should say it. You know—pray for wisdom like it says in the Bible. James 3 says the wisdom of God is pure. If God's wisdom is pure and you answer with His wisdom, then you're home-free, Bro. Then after you've taken care of first things first, sit down and write that note—and no more worrying.

"That's easy enough—I guess," Andrew said.

"About the note, Andrew, sometimes it's wise not to say too much. Once those words leave your mouth you can never get them back. You write your note with all that in mind—and you'll do fine. Let me know how she receives it, okay?"

"Okay—thanks, Sis," Andrew said. "Thanks for your—well—advice. You know, sometimes you are wise beyond your years. Say, maybe you can meet her before we leave on the mission."

"Oh . . . so she's that special, huh?" Jennifer said, raising one brow and smiling.

"Jen!" Andrew said, growing loud and serious. "Com'on, we're going to be late for the Captain's meeting."

Why does Jennifer tease me so much about this new girl? All I want to do is to encourage her for doing a good job—but Jen—she always has to make a big deal out of something little . . . . Oh well, I guess she is just being a sister. She did give good advice, though—she said to pray for wisdom because the wisdom God gives is pure. Why didn't I think of that? Jen's always one step ahead of me. How do I begin? Maybe I should just write out my prayer. I'll give it a shot.

Dear Lord, I need wisdom to know how to speak to the new girl. You say to ask for wisdom, and You will give it—this is Cadet Andrew asking for wisdom. In Jesus' name, Amen.

Well, Diary, how did I do?

Later,
Andrew

97

You decide! Did Jennifer give good advice to Andrew? If you said Yes, then you understand something about knowing how to say the right things to others. God tells us to ask for wisdom about everything, but it is especially important when it comes to our speech. If we want to have speech that doesn't hurt and is edifying, we need to ask God for His wisdom before we speak.

Jennifer shared an important truth about God's wisdom that could help your conversation with others. Underline the entire statement Jennifer made when she said something about God's wisdom being pure. Then turn to the passage in James, which she mentioned, and find the exact verse which states the same idea. Write the verse reference on the line below:

_____

Have you prayed for God's wisdom in your speech lately? Think about someone whom you might have offended with your speech. Have your words lacked encouragement or purity? Right now, make a commitment to ask God for His wisdom in your conversations with others this week.

Cadet Challenge 11.1

James 3:2 (NKJV)

Write the verse in the space and circle all the words in the word puzzle.

C L I H K V G W Z Z M W U D U B E G L T O N J T
N X D U B M J C R S A D E G B I R T Y O Y N R E
F S J U V H R D P W L Y F L Y O J J C R A K D L
X K O O S T K F G K L Z O W A V K R R X P H J D
D Z O S L A H D Y E H E Z N B J N A O I U R W R
H N S T Y W O E Q G J O E A T N M F T H Q N J G
T C E F R E P R R U A Q V H I S L O M O N Y A Y
J S L X N M V B K V U D T N I F L A A Q P P P X
R D O E S G M N I Q X R U P D O N Z F Q B A W N
D O T A K Q W B P X L F Y T G R N A H M A N Y W
X I U A B L E R E N X S S E V Z A O C I U H K O
H Z R Z A Y R F T E N K I A H C I H E U E J Y R
U I S M D U D H D E M F N W M Y N D U O L Z K D
P R Y O K S I X P C S Y E D P D Q D T H B O F O
O J J M E N L A E R O R W J P F T O L L M H Y I
H K R Q G L T P Z N Q L L A Y E C B H X U D S M
E T J S J C D J E B B J T A L V R J W E T S I Y
J E L C C J G I E J P K G O Q H B M R E S L T W
V F O Y Q R W M R A U K H D B J W Z R W W C M X
Z O A L H Z W K X B Y W L W W N C Q I J G N K S
M B U I T I F L W A M E L B M U T S Z L B I Z B
C I Q O Y Q R F N I O V N I F E A R C P A J W Z
V P A I C G B O D Y Z P O B H M S T P Z I V G G

Cadet Challenge 11.2

Read the references and write what the tongue can do. Then place a star next to the references that say what good the tongue can do.

References	The Tongue Can . . .
Psalm 5:9	
Psalm 35:28	
Psalm 12:3	
Psalm 15:3	
Psalm 37:30	
Psalm 34:13	
Psalm 51:14	
Psalm 52:2	
Proverbs 16:17	
Matthew 15:18	
James 3:5	
Psalm 119:172	
James 3:8	

Obeying or Disobeying

Who am I to obey?

What are the consequences when I disobey God?

Who was obedient and disobedient in the Bible?

How can I obey more consistently?

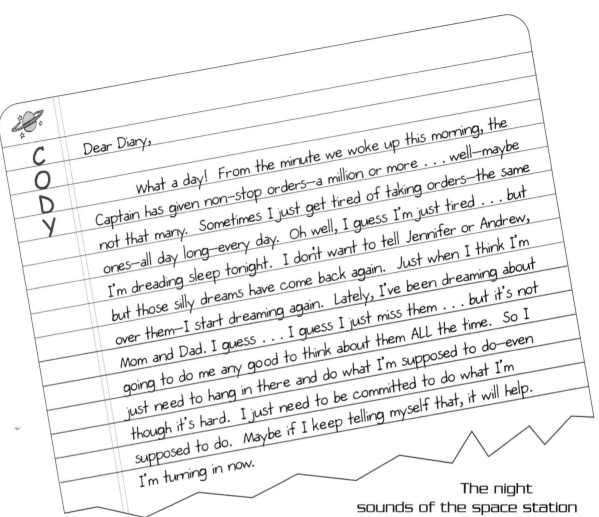

**C
O
D
Y**

Dear Diary,

What a day! From the minute we woke up this morning, the Captain has given non-stop orders—a million or more . . . well—maybe not that many. Sometimes I just get tired of taking orders—the same ones—all day long—every day. Oh well, I guess I'm just tired . . . but I'm dreading sleep tonight. I don't want to tell Jennifer or Andrew, but those silly dreams have come back again. Just when I think I'm over them—I start dreaming again. Lately, I've been dreaming about Mom and Dad. I guess . . . I guess I just miss them . . . but it's not going to do me any good to think about them ALL the time. So I just need to hang in there and do what I'm supposed to do—even though it's hard. I just need to be committed to do what I'm supposed to do. Maybe if I keep telling myself that, it will help. I'm turning in now.

The night sounds of the space station Orion were at their peak. At first, the whizzing and pinging that broke the silence of space kept everyone awake. But now the crew was accustomed to it, and nothing seemed to rob their sleep—except Cody's occasional nightmares. Cody drifted in and out of his dreams, all the while clutching his shiny set of Cadet's Wings. He was the youngest Cadet ever to be presented with wings after earning flight status.

"Dad, come back," he mumbled in his sleep. "I'm just a kid and I don't think I can do what you're asking."

In the dream, Cody's father had a proud, tender look on his face—and he was smiling at him. "I know, son," he said, comforting Cody, "but you are the one your mom and I have the most confidence in, even though you are the youngest. We've never expected anything of you that we weren't confident you're capable of accomplishing. The Lord has blessed each of you children. Remember, it's never wrong to do what's right, no matter what the circumstances are. Do what your authorities ask you to do."

The next morning Cody was awakened by the clunking sounds of the 'bots outside on the hull making their usual rounds checking for air leaks and meteoroid damage. Not sure he'd really been dreaming, he walked to the wall safe. Opening it revealed a pair of time-dulled bronze space wings. The wreath above the Federation shield encompassed a small star acknowledging the wearer to be Command Pilot qualified with combat experience.

"Dad's wings," Cody thought, remembering his dream. "So what if it was a dream. It was so good to see him again, and I will fulfill the mission with the Lord's help. I will do what I am asked to do—and I'll try not to complain about the orders any more."

"Hey, Jen," Cody called out. "Wait up."

"Hurry up before the rush for breakfast," she said, glancing over her shoulder as she trotted down the tube to the dining facility. "Andrew's probably already there and he's saving a place for us."

Catching up to match her speed, Cody told her about his dream. He ended with, ". . . and even if I am so young, you and Andrew will be with me, right? I mean, this is something we've just got to do—I mean we've got to just do it. Besides, God doesn't want us to keep our talents and gifts for our own ambitions."

Jennifer looked at him approvingly. "No problem with me. You know, Cody, Andrew and I have always known that we'd stick together as a family no matter what. Once we're underway and we break open the sealed orders, there is no turning back. We've always been committed to follow those orders and do what we have to do. We know you'll do your part."

Joining Andrew at a booth next to an observation window, the three of them watched Earth slowly moving under them as they ate. At times the conversation drifted to the subject of their missing parents.

"I can't help but wonder," Andrew pondered quietly, "that Mom and Dad may have been kidnapped by the so-called astro-pirates!"

Jennifer nodded in agreement.

"Astro-pirates!" Cody exclaimed. "What in the world are you . . .?

"Well, we've always felt that was a possibility," Jennifer interrupted. "Astro-pirates have been raiding interplanetary supply ships for years now. They might have mistaken Mom's research ship for a freighter."

"Hmmm . . . interesting idea. In spite of Dad's great combat skills, their ship just wasn't equipped defensively like the probes and insertion team ships are," said Cody.

"If we've been selected for a seemingly impossible job, our commanders must have known what they were doing," Andrew added. Maybe these astro-pirates, or whatever they are, will force us to get back to the strong principles that the founders established in the beginning."

"Even back in Bible times, God raised up judges to bring His people back to doing right," Jennifer interjected. "Maybe the astro-pirates are like being raided by modern-day Philistines."

"Yeah," Cody agreed, gleefully punching the air with his fists. "Maybe if I could be Samson and punch them all out into a decaying orbit around a black hole, then we'd get rid of them for good!"

"Oh, Cody," moaned Andrew, "I think you'd better choose a better judge to model."

"Why?" countered Cody, "Samson really knocked some people around the planet."

"Cody!" Jennifer scolded.

"Well, he did." Cody said.

"But at what cost?" Andrew continued. "He started off well, but was constantly disobeying God. Sure, God used Him to do some amazing things, but Samson didn't look different from your average person really. The movies on video microchips have made him into an imaginary hero."

"The Lord did give Samson his strength back—one last time in the end—but how much better for him and his people if he would have obeyed the Lord ALL his life," Jennifer concluded. "Andrew's right! Why don't you pattern yourself after . . . uhhh . . . Gideon? He was the youngest child just like you—and also somewhat fearful."

Jennifer continued, "He obeyed the Lord despite God's command to do incredible things. He did what was right and wasn't afraid to show his confidence. He didn't need a big army, only a small committed group, almost insignificant in number, just like us in comparison to the possible astro-pirate hordes."

"God gets all the credit that way, doesn't He?" Cody asked.

"As He should," Andrew said. "Obey God, do it His way and watch the blessings; or disobey God, do it your own way and live a life of regrets. Even if you do it your way, God's plan will still be accomplished, but at a terrible cost—as our judge Samson realized—but too late."

Just then the sun flashed over the blue horizon of Earth's oceans. It seemed to mark the beginning of a new day. For Cody, it symbolized new opportunities to choose the right path and walk in the Lord's Will.

. . . I liked today. It was good to have some time with my big bro and sister. Wow! Now I sound like Jennifer-calling Andrew "bro." I guess she's rubbing off on me. Well, that's okay-even though she IS a girl. I need to be more like Jennifer, anyway-her commitment to follow orders no matter what. Man, she's totally committed! Maybe I am fearful like Gideon was, but I can still obey and God CAN use me. Andrew said something about "do it God's way and He blesses, but do it my way and live a life of regrets." I'd rather have the blessings!

Signing off,

Cody

Cody liked the things his brother and sister said. Jennifer's commitment to follow orders encouraged him and gave him strength. And Andrew's insights on the consequences of obeying and disobeying gave him something to think about.

But what about you? Are you committed to following God's commands? How about your parents' requests, your teacher's instruction or classroom rules? Would you rather, like Cody, have the blessings—or would you rather live a life of regrets?

God gives you a choice: to walk in obedience no matter what, or to walk in disobedience. This week we will study two judges in Israel's history to compare and contrast their choices. We will see how those choices affected consequences—both good and bad. Keep in mind that choosing to obey God brings blessings, but continual disobedience brings regrets. Which will you choose?

Cadet Challenge 12.1

Use the verbs to help you fill in the verses.

" _____

_____ are not _____

_____

_____ pulling down _____

_____ , casting down _____

_____

_____ exalts itself _____

_____

_____ , bringing every _____

_____

_____ , and being ready to punish

_____

_____ is fulfilled."

Cadet Challenge 12.2

Who and What Are We Supposed to Obey?

Study the passages below and write who and what we are supposed to obey.
Find the one we are not supposed obey.

References	Who / What	Obey / Disobey
Colossians 3:20		
2 Thessalonians 3:14		
1 Peter 4:17		
Psalm 119:4		
Romans 6:12		
Hebrews 13:17		
Deuteronomy 11:13		
Proverbs 25:12		
Acts 5:29		

Depending on the Holy Spirit

Who is the Holy Spirit?

What does the Spirit do?

How does the Holy Spirit guide?

How can I learn to depend on Him?

JENNIFER

Dear Diary,
I am really coming to respect and trust Captain Callahan . . . a lot. I guess it's because he is so wise. The Captain always seems to know just the right time to steer us out of trouble—we could have been doomed. It's like the Admiral gives the orders, but the Captain makes it all happen—and they work as a team.
One thing I wish, though—that my little brother would stop teasing me about the time when I thought the Captain was too bossy. He was always telling us what to do and then showing us how to do it—but to tell you the truth, Captain Callahan has been a great guide through every step of our mission—I just had to learn to depend on him instead of my own smarts—intuition as Andrew calls it.

All four "private channel" message indicators lit up at the same time. The four officers who were in various stages of rest, work, study or play responded quickly. One doesn't just glance at a personal page in space and then go on as if it weren't important. Every message is vitally important.

Cody was the most startled. He'd only received one such call before, and it was when his mom and his dad had disappeared. Reluctantly, he keyed the code to receive a visual along with an audible report.

"Whew!" he breathed out gratefully. "It's not an emergency." He lowered his sleeve hiding the small com unit on his wrist and wondered why Admiral Haynes had requested a private meeting at 0745 the next morning—and why no one was to be told, not even Andy or Sis.

The other com units had displayed identical orders, except that Captain Callahan's time was 0730, Andrew's was 0735 and Jennifer's time to appear was 0740.

Captain Callahan was ushered into the Admiral's office by two security officers and then directed to the Admiral's XO. The executive officer escorted the Captain into Admiral Haynes' sterile briefing room where highly classified conversations usually took place.

"Thanks for your time, Cal, I know you are about to launch. Your assistance here repairing the damage to the Orion space station was most appreciated. Sorry it delayed your mission."

"My crew was glad to help," the Captain answered, pleased to be privately addressed in such a familiar way by the Fleet Admiral. "We had the skills and could afford the time because of a wide launch window."

"I'm going to meet my grandchildren one at a time in the outer office, then send them back to you," the Admiral said as he turned to wait for Andrew. "I'm entrusting them into your hands."

"Good morning, sir," Andrew saluted crisply, looking around the empty office. He had approached the door 30 seconds before he was to enter and now stood before the Admiral's desk at exactly 0735.

"At ease, Andy. I just wanted to wish my eldest grandson a successful launch and future mission. My daughter—your mother—would be so proud of you right now. I'm proud as well. The Lord has been so good to your family."

Andrew's throat started to feel tight—and he couldn't talk. He was overcome with emotion.

"You're the man of the family now," Admiral Haynes continued. "Please be careful in your responsibilities, and bring your whole family back to us safe and sound. You have the skills; we'll give you the resources. I'll meet with you in the briefing room momentarily."

Andrew shuffled off like a zombie, wondering what was going on. He snapped out of it when he saw the Captain waiting there for him.

"Come in, Jenny," Admiral Haynes smiled. "I want to give you a personal bit of encouragement before you launch. You'll have to grow up fast, acting as a mother at times to Cody and as an officer with Andy. Your mother would be so happy to see how you've matured. Bring her back to all of us soon. I'll join you in the briefing room in a few minutes."

"Hi Cody, my boy," the Admiral said, offering Cody a high five. Cody bounded to him and they smacked their hands together.

"Tomorrow we get to launch! I'm so excited!" Cody blurted out, his eyes gleaming brightly.

"That's right, Cody, and I want to make the mission special for you. Your father left me an extra set of his wings. I was to officially pin them on you when we both felt that you were ready. I think now would be the perfect time."

Cody's eyes grew wide.

"Just like in my dreams of Dad," he managed to get out. "I'll try to live up to what they stand for, sir," Cody said as he drew himself to attention and saluted smartly.

"I know you will, Cody. The three of you are the best we've ever produced through the Academy. Let's go to the briefing room. I want you to meet with some special people."

Admiral Haynes positioned himself in front of the group now sitting on the sofa. He spoke softly and deliberately, glancing from one to the other—then he focused on Captain Callahan.

"I'm sorry I can't go with you on your mission. I've personally selected you, Captain Callahan, as a trusted friend to watch over this mission. You and I will be in constant contact. And Cadets, you treat your Captain as though he were me. What he says and what he asks of you comes from me."

They all nodded solemnly.

"Share your needs with Captain Callahan. He will in turn approach me, and I will meet with the Federation's Inner Council, the only ones who have seen your sealed orders other than me. Later, when you return, you will have direct access to the Inner Council, a privilege that only the Chancellor and I now share!"

Admiral Haynes rose, opened his arms and beckoned them to come closer. They all stood in a circle with their arms on each other's shoulders then bowed their heads in silence.

"Lord God of Heaven and earth, as I send my children off on a dangerous, yet exciting mission, may they see Your purposes in it. Grant them the strength to press on and the wisdom to carefully discern the proper path. Be with their Captain as he provides comfort and guidance in times of need. In Jesus' name, Amen."

No one said anything until the Admiral broke the silence. "Cadets, depend on your Captain. He will guide your every decision!"

Boy, am I relieved. I know Andrew is, too. I think even Cody is finally at peace—well maybe not so scared— about the mission. But then, who wouldn't be feeling pretty good with a Captain like ours. He is A-O.K.! What great news to hear that we will be in close contact with someone who loves us and our family—my grandfather—I mean, the Admiral.

Later,

Jen

Why was Jennifer feeling so relieved? Why did she think that Cody was also at peace about the mission? Because the Admiral had assigned Captain Callahan, an intelligent, dependable, decision-maker, to be personally responsible for the Cadets' welfare. The Cadets felt secure under the Captain's careful guidance. They were comforted to know they could trust the person in charge. They could depend on the Captain; he had proven himself. If anyone could guide the mission to success, he could.

This is how the Holy Spirit works in our lives. God the Father has assigned the third person of the Trinity to be our comforter and guide. As we cooperate with Him we will live wisely and peacefully, throughout the mission of our lives. If we resist the Holy Sprit's control of our lives, then everything will be out of order. The question is this: Are you allowing the Holy Spirit to control you?

Cadet Challenge 13.1

The Holy Spirit
Who Was He and What Did He Do?

Use the punctuation marks to help you write the verse. Clue: Every line begins with the word "He."

"However, when

_____, _____, _____,

_____, for

_____, but whatever

_____, and

_____."

John 16:13

Cadet Challenge 13.2

Are You Allowing the Holy Sprit to Control Your Life?

Mark the percentage of time that you can answer yes.

Question	0	10	20	30	40	50	60	70	80	90	100%
1 Do you believe the Holy Spirit is a person?											
2 Do you believe the Holy Spirit is God?											
3 Do you know the Holy Spirit is living inside you?											
4 Do you pray daily that He will guide you?											
5 Do you know for sure that you are a Christian?											
6 Do you often feel guilty when you disobey God?											
7 Do you ask God to help you know how to pray?											
8 Do you understand the Bible when you read it?											
9 Do you know that you are going to Heaven?											
10 Do you avoid grieving the Holy Spirit?											
11 Do you avoid quenching the Holy Spirit?											
12 Do you use your talents to serve God?											

Find the average percentage for your total score and write it here: _____

Committing to His Word

Why are God's words so important?

What is the truth about the Bible?

What does the Bible do for me?

How does God's Word benefit me?

JENNIFER

Dear Diary,

It is 0300 hours, and we just boarded our super-secret, stealth space-cruiser. We all agreed with Captain Callahan that it was best to board during the crew's normal sleep time—although losing sleep is NOT my favorite thing to do—BELIEVE ME! All I can say is—Captain Callahan has never steered us wrong before—so we must continue to trust his good judgment. One thing I don't understand is why He seems so concerned about Mom and Dad's Operating Manual. I know the Operating Manual is important—we all know that—but the Captain keeps warning us that if we don't follow the Manual exactly, it would be easy to get lost in space. Now that's a scary thought, and I just . . . uhhh . . . speaking of Captain Callahan and the Operating Manual, he is directing us to take our positions now and go through the instructions in the . . . uhhh . . . Operating Manual. I'd better go. Will write more later.

Andrew, Jennifer and Cody took their places at their consoles and began going over last-minute checklists while Captain Callahan, First Officer Bryant and Navigator James prepared their ship.

"Andrew, my legs are still shaking," Jennifer said with excitement. "I can hardly believe we're finally underway."

"I know what you mean, Sis, I'm a bit shaky myself," Andrew confessed. "Okay, Cody, begin sequencing the outer pod bay doors."

"Roger! Outer sequence commencing in five, four, three, two, one . . . engage!" Cody keyed in the final sequence to open the large hangar doors.

Ever so slowly the distant stars began peeking through the ever-widening crack as the large doors lumbered open. There was no sound in the vacuum of space, but the low rumbling vibrations betrayed their ponderous presence.

"Cadet Andrew, Captain Callahan here. We're clear of the station and our sensors indicate no traffic in this sector. Looks like we made a clean departure. You're clear to release your docking clamps and proceed to rendezvous Alpha-One as planned."

Andrew pulsed the ion drive thrusters and the ship, already as dark as night itself, slipped into the absolute blackness of space. Except for its massive bulk blocking the stars, no one could ever even know it was there. Then, all of a sudden, it totally disappeared by lighting up its black hull with tiny points of light that perfectly imitated the location of the very stars it was blocking.

"What an incredible sight!" exclaimed Captain Callahan. "Actually, what an incredible 'nothing' since I can't see anything now! Your mother did an excellent job designing the ship, Cadet Andrew. You have absolutely no signal signature whatsoever except for the residual ion plasma pulse from pushing off."

"Exactly what we had hoped for, Captain," said Jennifer, holding the com. "Proceeding to Alpha-One. Initiating radio silence, maintaining stealth mode. Over and out."

"Roger that, Seeker," responded the captain, "Guardian-One clear."

"Okay, Cody, I want you and Jennifer to hover as close to the Guardian as possible," Andrew commanded quietly. "I want to be able to count the rivets in the hull plating and still be undetected. Let's see what Mom's ship is really capable of doing."

"The ship's Operating Manual was written by both Dad and Mom and has everything we need to know about her capabilities," Jennifer pondered audibly. "I think it was very appropriate that Mom named her ship 'Seeker,' especially now that they are missing and we're being sent to find them."

"We'll be putting every system to the test," said Andrew. "It looks like the stealth mode is working well according to the Manual. We've been spiraling around the Guardian and they don't even know we're only a few meters away from her hull. It's nice to have a manual we can so completely count on—a source of reliable information as we continue the mission."

"You know, Andrew, we can have total confidence in Mom and Dad's Operating Manual because we have total confidence in them. It's like a letter from their hearts and minds now that they can't be with us to help.

"Yeah, Captain Callahan is our guardian now. It's interesting that his ship is named Guardian," Cody added, looking up from his console. "I wonder if Admiral Haynes had anything to do with that?"

Guardian's main thrusters began radiating their warm-up signature and Andrew gently directed Seeker away, aligning it with the proposed trajectory toward Alpha-One intercept. There was a bright flash of ignition and Guardian, at first slowly and then increasingly faster, pulled ahead on its initial course insertion burn.

"According to the Operating Manual we need to allow Guardian to accelerate way ahead and then practice catching up as quickly as Mom's notes say we can," Cody advised Andrew.

"Good idea, Cody," Andrew responded. "We both know what the answer will be, but proving it will build our confidence in Dad and Mom's documents."

"Jen, you keep an eye on the thrust initiators and make sure they are synchronized with the fuel flow. That new fuel has ten times the thrust of anything else ever used," Andrew cautioned.

"Everything is right on the numbers—the way the Manual says it's supposed to be, Andrew."

"Looks good from nav," Cody added.

"Okay, automatic sequencer set. Strap down hard everyone," Andrew commanded. "This is going to be a military departure with full jets and blasters on max. Remember, keep a tight gut and take your breaths in short, quick pants or you'll never get enough air exchanged. Keep your tongue in, your teeth clenched and your helmet against the head rest."

Wham! The solid slam from the back felt as though they'd been rear-ended by a renegade nickel-iron meteor. Their eyeballs pushing back into sockets caused the cadets to see stars, far brighter than the real ones outside the hull. The vibrations were so violent that the cadets felt as though they were getting a free "power massage" from canned thunder.

The physical bashing finally ceased. They were all surprised to watch Guardian flash past as though it were standing still in space.

"We'll beat them to the intercept for sure now," Cody said growing in excitement.

"We're still right on the numbers, Andrew," Jennifer reported.

"Good!" Andrew said.

"Captain Callahan was right again. Without this Operating Manual, we'd be . . . well . . . lost," Jennifer said. "But with the Operating Manual, and God's grace, we'll find Mom and Dad and bring them home."

"Yep! It sure is great to be able to trust that what we're reading in the Manual is 100% accurate. Our lives depend on these figures being correct."

Some time passed before further instructions were given. The drone of the engines was the only noise heard in the quietness of the night. Cody was the first to break the silence.

"The Bible's kinda' like an operating manual," said Cody, thinking out loud. "One hundred percent accurate . . . necessary to our lives . . . and we can trust it all the time."

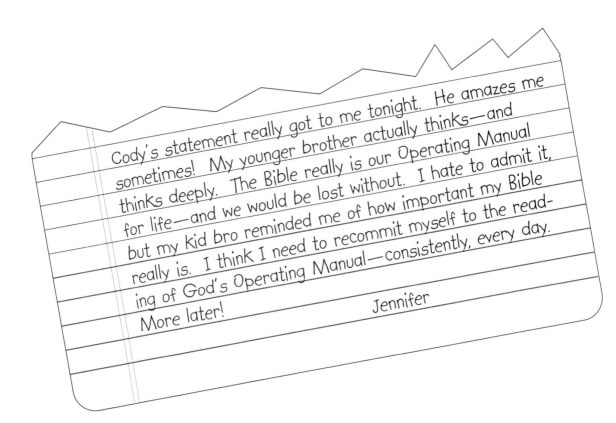

Cody's statement really got to me tonight. He amazes me sometimes! My younger brother actually thinks—and thinks deeply. The Bible really is our Operating Manual for life—and we would be lost without. I hate to admit it, but my kid bro reminded me of how important my Bible really is. I think I need to recommit myself to the reading of God's Operating Manual—consistently, every day. More later!   Jennifer

Have you, like Jennifer, forgotten something very important? She knew she should read the Word of God every day, but something happened to distract her and she omitted the most important activity of the day.

Before you get too comfortable criticizing Jennifer's problem, ask yourself these questions:

- Is this the same problem I have sometimes?
- Do I omit reading God's Word because I am too busy doing what I want to do?
- Do I omit reading God's Word because I am too lazy?

Many people intend to read God's Word every day, but things seem to get in their way. They choose other priorities, other things that seem more important at the time. How can you avoid this sin? Fully commit to His Word. Read the Bible every day to find out how to live in ways that please God. Jennifer got back on track when she made a wise choice to daily read the Word of God. Do you need to make the same wise decision?

Cadet Challenge 14.1

What's the Question,
Answer and Exclamation?

Write the question, answer and exclamation in the appropriate speech boxes.

Psalm 119:9-10

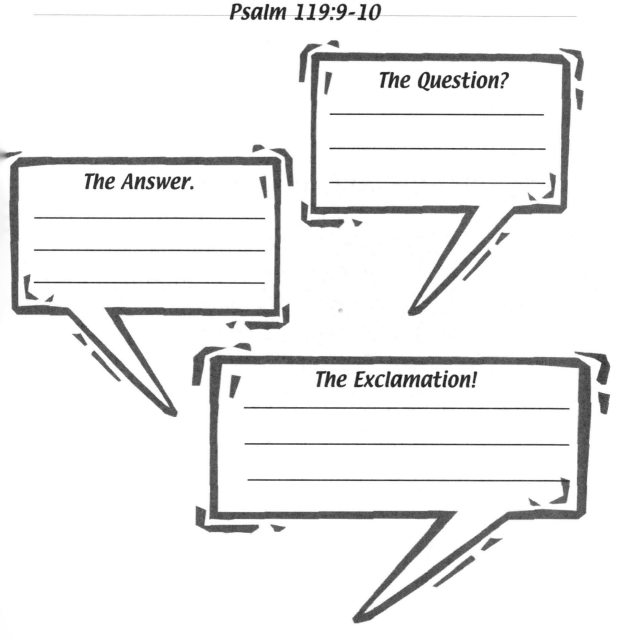

The Question?

_____

_____

_____

The Answer.

_____

_____

_____

The Exclamation!

_____

_____

_____

Cadet Challenge 14.2

Who Said What about the Word of God?

Fill in the blanks from each person's statement that gives the truth about the Word of God.

1
Proverbs 30:5

Agur said, "Every _____ of God is _____."

2
Luke 4:4

Jesus said, "Man shall not _____ by bread alone, but by every _____ of God."

3
Hebrews 4:12

The author said, "For the _____ of God is _____ and _____, a discerner of the _____ and intents of the _____."

4
1 Peter 1:23

Peter said, "having been _____ again, through the _____ of God which _____ and abides forever,"

5
2 Samuel 22:31

David said, "The _____ of the Lord is _____."

6
Isaiah 55:10–11

Isaiah said, "It (God's Word) shall not return to Me void, but it shall_____ what I please, and it shall _____ in the thing for which I sent it."

124

15

Balancing the Christian Life

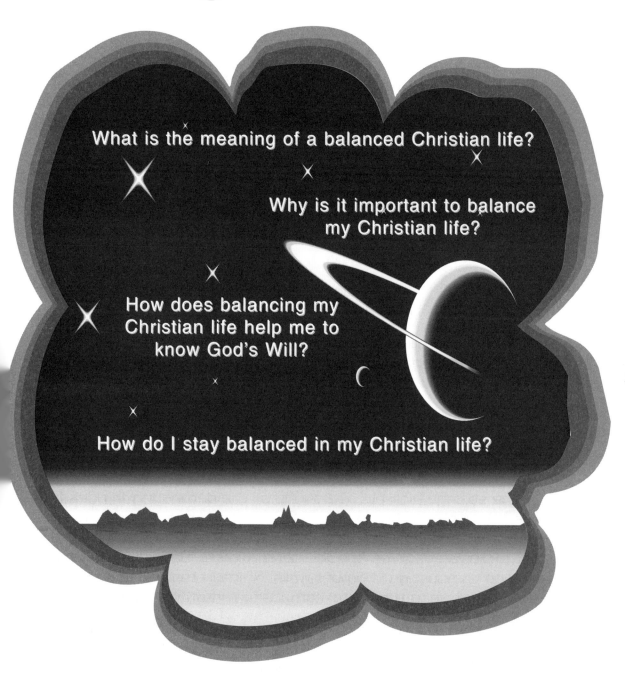

What is the meaning of a balanced Christian life?

Why is it important to balance my Christian life?

How does balancing my Christian life help me to know God's Will?

How do I stay balanced in my Christian life?

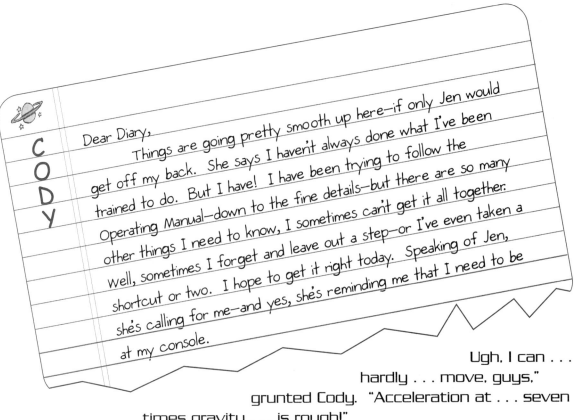

C
O
D
Y

Dear Diary,
     Things are going pretty smooth up here—if only Jen would get off my back. She says I haven't always done what I've been trained to do. But I have! I have been trying to follow the Operating Manual—down to the fine details—but there are so many other things I need to know, I sometimes can't get it all together. Well, sometimes I forget and leave out a step—or I've even taken a shortcut or two. I hope to get it right today. Speaking of Jen, she's calling for me—and yes, she's reminding me that I need to be at my console.

Ugh. I can . . . hardly . . . move, guys," grunted Cody. "Acceleration at . . . seven times gravity . . . is rough!"

"You should have . . . exercised a little longer . . . in the gym, Cody . . . to toughen up . . . your body for this . . . mission," Jennifer replied.

"I did work out . . . for hours and hours," said Cody.

"Maybe for the first five days. But what about . . . the last 20 days . . . of training, Cody?" Jennifer said.

The strange high-pitched sound of the detonating Tri-odek fuels traveled through the hull as the merciless hammering continued aft in the power plant. Incredible shock waves were generated by the violent explosion of three special fuel mixtures. Detonations hammered the combustion chamber walls, which in turn conducted the sound directly along the metal-composite materials of the hull.

The combustion chambers were actually located inside the hull. Baffles hid the searing hot gases, so blinding in their blue-white glare and heat signature that they would instantly betray the ship's position.

"The sound level during acceleration . . . would be unbearable . . . if the hull couldn't absorb the vibrations," Andrew managed to get out. "It's the composite materials . . . of carbon fiber, epoxy and ceramic . . . that protect us."

Suddenly the violence ceased and all was deathly still. They'd reached mid-course, where the ship could be turned around, then reverse thrust would slow them down to a standstill near the rendezvous point.

"Andrew?" Jennifer paused. "This would be a good time to test our acceleration-deceleration gel capsules. We could delay the braking phase for a while and then push it up to 80% max to see how we handle 15 gravities in the caps."

"Excellent idea, Jen. Go for it!" Andrew floated out of his command pilot's seat to check the navigation points with Cody.

"This is really comforting, Jen, we're still right on the numbers. Great nav job, Cody," Andrew said, patting him on the back.

Cody started floating away from the force of that gentle touch, having already loosened his harness.

"Hey, wait, I lost my grip on the console!" Cody laughed at his own comedy performance while grasping thin air trying to get an anchor hold on anything within reach. "I tell you I'm not used to space yet!"

Jennifer frowned. "Oh Cody!" she scolded. "You know better than to take your hands off the console."

With the thrusters off, they were drifting free in space, yet were moving at hundreds of thousands of kilometers per hour. Andrew could have adjusted the thrust to apply a one-gravity acceleration or deceleration, but he wanted to keep the computations easy for this next test.

"Hey, I know what buttons to push," Cody barked.

"You know what buttons to push, Cody, but you also have to get used to space—just like you got used to the Academy—just like you got used to the regimen of school—just like you got used to dealing with the senior cadets and—just like you must get used to all the other changes that come in life," lectured Jennifer.

"I'm doing okay," Cody assured her.

"Yeah, you're doing—okay," she agreed. "But you just can't concentrate on one thing only, Cody, or else you'll miss other important things. In fact, all of life must be balanced. You learn how to do something—or you learn what's right—and then you learn how to APPLY it in practice. It's not just your head knowledge that counts."

"I know, Sis. I believe you've said the same thing to me before—and another time before that," Cody said, bugging his eyes at his sister.

Jennifer pretended not to notice that her comments had irritated her brother. "Of course we all make mistakes," she continued. "But being willing to correct ourselves is what counts in the long run. And those little corrections in our thoughts and actions are just one of the ways we know that God is building wisdom and discipline into our lives—and that's one of the ways we know we are balanced. B-a-l-a-n-c-e, Cody. I'm talking about balancing what you know to do with what you actually do."

"Okay, guys. Climb into your protective suits, and into the capsules we go," Andrew ordered.

With the deceleration programmed into the computers, the three of them climbed into their respective capsules and allowed the gel to totally surround them.

"Hey, this suit is like being inside a balloon covered with slime. It's weird," Cody said as the gel rose above his waist.

Soon they were each floating in the center of a protective gel that would evenly distribute the forces of deceleration and acceleration, thus minimizing the crushing stress on their bodies. The whole ship shuddered. The violent release of incredible power stored in the chemical structure of the Tri-odek fuel labored unrelentingly in its efforts to slow the fantastic speed of the stealth cruiser. The Cadets were thankful that the system worked as designed.

"We are here!" Andrew reported.

The gel drained. Peeling off the protective suits, they each returned to their respective consoles and computed the current status of the ship. They were at intercept Alpha-One. In max stealth the Guardian would never know they were already in position, so they were eager to test their stealth capabilities again.

"Guardian One, this is Seeker One. Do you copy?"

Captain Callahan jerked in total surprise. "Where did that come from?" he asked his com officer.

"Looks like they beat us here, Sir, although I can't detect them on any band, visual, infrared or radar," Officer James stated. "I knew that ship was special, but this is fantastic! They're not even occluding any stars, so there is no black shape to look for either."

"We're ready to transfer across to unseal the orders, Captain," Andrew said as he secured the transfer tube to their hull plates.

"Welcome aboard, Cadets. That's quite a ship you have there." The Captain's comments were genuine after witnessing its recent achievement. "Let's all head to the briefing room."

After the debriefing, Andrew asked, "Are these orders correct, Captain? If this information is true, it is absolutely incredible!"

"It looks like Dad and Mom are being held for ransom!" Jennifer exclaimed.

A look of panic came over Cody; he was speechless. Andrew and Jennifer put their arms around him.

Captain Callahan quietly walked over to the young Cadets and hugged them. "It will be okay, my young friends," he offered. "This is a part of growing stronger and wiser. We've got our orders and the full support of the Federation, especially Admiral Haynes. The intelligence gathered is correct—and it doesn't look good. But perhaps there is another way out for your mom and dad."

Boy, Jen really knows how to get to me. She did it again today! She keeps badgering me about being balanced or something. What is this balance anyway? If I follow the Operating Manual down to the letter, and forget some other things I've learned, then she says that I'm unbalanced. If I don't follow it enough, then she also says I'm unbalanced. I don't get it! I'm either unbalanced—or unbalanced. Am I that way in my Christian life, too?

Signing off,
Cody

Cody seems confused about what it means to balance his life. Have you ever had that problem? For example, have you ever wondered how much time you should spend on homework, on practicing the piano or kicking the soccer ball? Or do you question the amount of time you spend watching TV as opposed to cleaning your room? Do you ever wonder how much time you should spend reading your Bible and praying? If you've ever wondered about these things, then you are really wondering how to balance all the activities in your life.

You are faced with a multitude of choices every day—and many of them involve choosing between something good and something better. For example: A choice you might be facing after school is whether you should spend more time practicing the piano, or more time practicing soccer. Since you have committed yourself to learn how to play the piano, and also to be on a soccer team, you need to practice both. If you like one activity better than the other, then it will be difficult for you to stay balanced unless you discipline yourself to the task. Also, there might be times when you would need to spend more time on one than the other. Three good questions to ask yourself are:

- Have my parents put more of an emphasis or priority on one over the other?
- Has God given me an ability in one area over the other?
- Does one have more importance than the other right now? (For example, do you have a piano recital or a soccer tournament coming up for which you need more practice?)

If your answers favored piano, then it would be wise to practice the piano more than you practice soccer—and vice versa.

How balanced are you when you decide you must leave out reading God's Word because you want to spend all your time on athletics or music? If you answered "Not very balanced," then you answered correctly. Having a balanced approach in life means that we use our time wisely by setting priorities and sticking with them.

And what should our priorities be? Our number one priority should be that we seek God first. Reading and obeying God's Word, talking to Him through prayer, and asking Him for wisdom are all activities that help to balance our lives. They are the first things we should do if we want to balance our lives.

God's Son is our example in balancing our Christian lives. This week you will see how Jesus Christ balanced His life at age twelve. His example will give you a pattern to follow as you work to balance your own life.

Cadet Challenge 15.1

Can You Write the Words in the Appropriate Boxes?

Write each word and each punctuation mark of the memory verse in a box. Separate chapter, colon and verse. Then write the verse on the lines.

? ! : Matthew 6:33 : ! ?

Cadet Challenge 15.2

How Do You Know That Jesus' Life Was Balanced?

Write the answers from Luke 2:39-52. Include references.

How do you know that . . .

Jesus was growing spiritually?

verses:

Jesus' mother and Joseph were trying to follow God?

verses:

Jesus' mother and Joseph cared for Him?

verses:

Jesus was a special Boy?

verses:

Cadet Challenge 15.2 (continued)

Jesus understood what God's Will was for Him?

verse: _____
     _____
     _____

Jesus' mother and Joseph did not fully understand God's plan

for Jesus? _____

verse: _____
     _____
     _____

Jesus obeyed His mother and Joseph? _____

verse: _____
     _____
     _____

Jesus was balancing His life in ways pleasing to God?

verses: _____
      _____

Resisting Peer Pressure

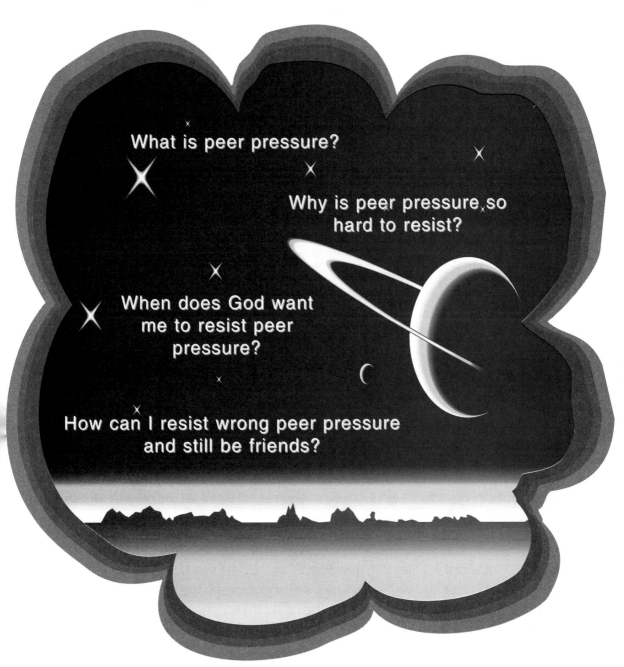

What is peer pressure?

Why is peer pressure so hard to resist?

When does God want me to resist peer pressure?

How can I resist wrong peer pressure and still be friends?

Dear Diary,

Captain Callahan says we are going to reunite with some of the other crewmembers today. I wish I could say I was looking forward to it—I'm actually a little nervous, especially if Trey is in the group. At the Academy he was the leader of the pack. Whatever Trey said to do, most of the guys did—even when it wasn't right! Well, of course I didn't follow along—and Jennifer and Cody didn't either—but it was hard to resist. Trey made us feel small in front of the others at the Academy—like big zeros. I sure hope he's not part of the other crew. Cody—he's so sensitive these days—I don't know if he is strong enough to resist a person like Trey right now. The pressure might be too strong for my little bro.

A N D R E W

"I miss Mom and Dad so much," Cody groaned as he entered Andrew's room.

Andrew covered his diary quickly before Cody could see what he had written. Jennifer appeared at the door.

"Oh, uhhh . . . Hi. It's going to be all right, Little Bro." Andrew said, putting his hand on Cody's shoulder. "We'll work together as a team with the Guardian's crew. You watch! We'll snatch Mom and Dad right out from under the noses of those pirate kidnappers."

"That's right," Jennifer added, "because we have the better ships, the better crews—and higher purposes. We would be willing to sacrifice—at least, more than a bunch of pirates would. We'd better get going before we're late for the big "reunion," as Captain calls it."

The Cadets headed for the recreational facilities in one of the forward bays. Captain Callahan felt it was necessary to get the two crews acquainted again after they had worked separately during the repairs to the space station Orion. Each team had learned to appreciate one another's skills and gifts, but so much work was required that there had been little time to forge lasting relationships.

"Hey Andrew, over here!" shouted one of the other pilots. "I want you on my side for this set."

Andrew glanced toward the back of the rec bay and saw one of his Academy classmates—it was Trey. Andrew groaned silently.

"Yeah, I'll be right over," Andrew replied. Andrew glanced at Jennifer and then Officer James. Slowly he turned to walk toward Trey.

"Is something the matter, Andrew?" Officer James questioned.

"No, sir," Andrew said over his shoulder.

"Cody, you're just in time to join the game and even the odds for me," Officer James whispered and winked. "Jennifer, you can keep score since I don't trust Maintenance."

"Watch it, James, or we'll forget to calibrate the plasma constrictors on your nav gyros, and you'll end up in the center of the sun," one of the crewmembers teased.

"You could try, but my pal Cody here could do the comps in his head and probably do it faster than you could using your computer," Officer James challenged.

Captain Callahan, seated high above in an observation booth, watched the various crew interactions. He was particularly interested in the increasing hubbub at the back of the bay where some of the crewmembers had joined Trey. They were standing in a circle talking to Andrew. Andrew looked pale.

"Look guys, I don't need to do that to win. It would be a shallow victory anyway," Andrew shot back at his current teammates.

"What's the big deal? Everyone cuts corners now and then to get ahead," Trey said with a smirk on his face.

"Yeah, what's the big deal?" other crewmembers asked, looking at each other while snickering.

"Professionals don't do that—especially not if you're working in space at our speeds. You do it by the numbers and by the Operating Manual. You hope there is enough over-design to smooth out any slight errors," Andrew countered.

All the crewmembers knew that space ships only fly in straight lines in space, one thrust vector after another. They all knew the old-fashioned space movies were such a joke showing sharp curving attacks and escape paths using minimal power. Nevertheless, Andrew's peers were encouraging him to cheat by using shortcuts. Trey and some of the crewmembers kept pressing Andrew, but he held his ground.

"Don't even bother trying to convince me, guys. I made my mind up long ago on this one," Andrew said as he turned away.

"Looks like Andrew has his hands full with that crowd, doesn't it Officer Bryant?" Captain Callahan was staring at the group now, leaning on the table with his chin on his hand.

"He sure has, sir. But I've worked with Cadet Andrew—and he has strong convictions. I don't think they'll sway him on this one," Officer Bryant said.

Bryant was right to be confident about Andrew's resolve. Andrew had used the same technique to walk the straight line when he was in school. Andrew's parents had taught him how to react when certain members in his group wanted to do something that he thought was not right.

"I saw that!" Jennifer commented as Andrew joined her and Cody. "Don't tell me we're going to face this again—with Trey and his buddies, I mean."

"Looks like we are—but we're just gonna' have to be strong," Andrew said.

"And you were," said Jennifer. "You REALLY were."

"Yeah! You were, Andrew. I don't know if I could have answered like that," Cody said.

Officer James walked over to join the Cadets. "Cody, did anyone ever tell you that you have almost superhuman ability to plot nav intercepts and tactical approaches? It's a talent crucial to the success of our upcoming mission."

"Cody's the best," said Jennifer. "After Officer James—of course."

Captain Callahan descended the spiral stairs to the lower deck, and the crews all snapped to attention. "At ease everyone," he quickly said. "I think we've all appreciated the opportunity to relax and get acquainted again before the mission gets under way. But let's not forget why we're here. Some pretty nasty people have captured two of the Academy's finest scientists, and we are going to get them back!"

A cheer arose from the entire crowd. Cody and Jennifer gave each other a high five. Voices were so loud that Trey covered his ears, squinted and made a face; the other crewmembers laughed and did the same. Captain Callahan smiled, raised his hands to quiet the crowd and said, "Let's head back to our sleep quarters. We've got a long day ahead of us."

Trey was the first to leave, with the other crewmembers following close behind. The Cadets were last in line. The Captain caught Andrew by the sleeve. "I saw what happened tonight, son. I know it wasn't easy—but you did the right thing. You were following the Operating Manual's procedures to a T."

"Thank you, sir. I've had to stand alone before—and I'll have to do it again." Andrew smiled then walked away with Jennifer and Cody.

As everyone headed toward the sleep quarters, Captain Callahan reflected on the top-secret orders that he'd be discussing the next day with his crew. "We absolutely must be totally prepared in heart, mind and body—like Andrew. Some of us may not be coming back—and I don't want any of my crewmembers unprepared to meet their Maker," the Captain whispered under his breath.

My worst fears have come true! Trey Matthews was assigned to our mission. The Captain introduced us tonight—not that I needed to be reintroduced to Trey, 'cause I won't ever forget him from our days together at the Academy. Hopefully, I've learned better how to handle him. He's still the same Trey, still intimidating, still the B.M.O.C.—Big Man On Campus. I don't know why he gets to me, but he does. In fact, he gets to everyone! He puts a lot of pressure on everyone to do things his way, even when it's not the right thing to do. It's either Trey's way or no way.

When Trey's around, I need to stand firm for what's right. It's important for me to be a good example to the others. I think Jennifer won't be impressed or intimidated by Trey, but I'm not so sure about Cody. He's younger—and easier to influence.

Later,
Andrew

Have you ever known someone like Trey? Someone who puts pressure on you to do things that are not right? If not, you will probably meet someone like him in the future. The Treys are everywhere. That's why you need to know how to handle the pressure they can put on you. That pressure is called "peer pressure" because it comes to you through people close to your own age. They can be influential and persuasive. Although not all peer pressure is bad, much of the pressure can be negative and work against you. You need to grow in your ability to discern when peer pressure is bad and when it is good.

The peer pressure that Andrew faced from Trey obviously was not good. How did Andrew stand up to it? He kept his convictions! He did not budge from what he knew was right. It wasn't easy for Andrew to insist on following the Operating Manual when Trey and his crowd were snickering and trying to get him to cut corners. Nevertheless, Andrew stood for what he knew was right. He was not swayed by the group, even though he was made to feel stupid. He made up his mind beforehand that he would not take shortcuts—and he didn't.

When is peer pressure good? An example is when your peers influence you to make wise choices compatible with God's teaching in the Bible. Influencing others in healthy ways is positive peer pressure. That is why it's so important to choose your friends wisely. A good friend can help you choose God's ways. Pray that God will help you to resist the wrong peer pressure. Pray that He will help you grow in your discernment!

Cadet Challenge 16.1

== Proverbs 4:14–15 ==

Use your Bible to write the words of the verses in alphabetical order.
Then close your Bible and write the words in sentence order.

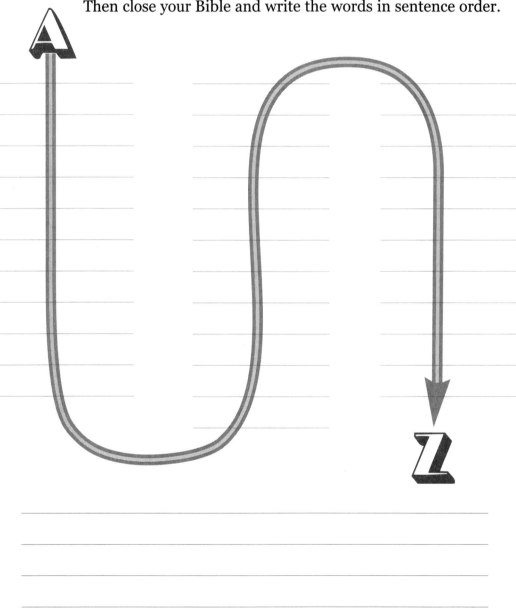

Cadet Challenge 16.2

Read each passage. Decide who was the minority and who made up the majority, and which side was right.

Passage	Minority	Majority	Who Was Wise?
1 Kings 18:20–39			
Numbers 13:1–3 14:1–12, 36–38			
Daniel 1:1–21			

Based on what you have read in Scripture, write True or False beside the following statements.

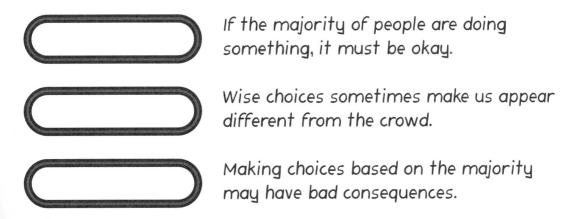

If the majority of people are doing something, it must be okay.

Wise choices sometimes make us appear different from the crowd.

Making choices based on the majority may have bad consequences.

143

Living Without Hypocrisy

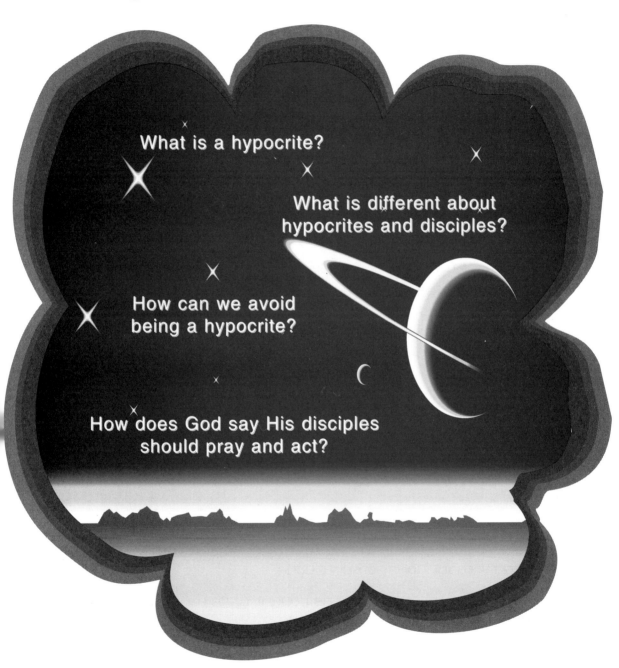

What is a hypocrite?

What is different about hypocrites and disciples?

How can we avoid being a hypocrite?

How does God say His disciples should pray and act?

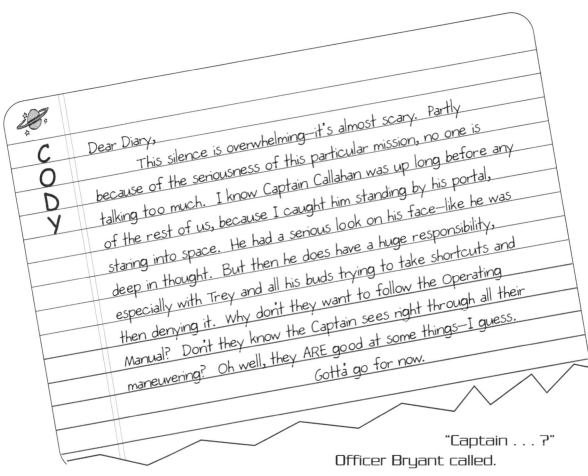

Dear Diary,

This silence is overwhelming—it's almost scary. Partly because of the seriousness of this particular mission, no one is talking too much. I know Captain Callahan was up long before any of the rest of us, because I caught him standing by his portal, staring into space. He had a serious look on his face—like he was deep in thought. But then he does have a huge responsibility, especially with Trey and all his buds trying to take shortcuts and then denying it. Why don't they want to follow the Operating Manual? Don't they know the Captain sees right through all their maneuvering? Oh well, they ARE good at some things—I guess. Gotta go for now.

"Captain . . . ?"
Officer Bryant called.

The Captain's thoughts were in another world. He could hardly imagine a time when commanders sent tens of thousands of their troops into hostile, life-threatening territory. Right now he was having such a hard time doing it with only a few dozen. The pain, sadness and loss for those left behind dulled only after years of healing.

"Captain, sir . . . ?" Officer Bryant repeated, finally getting through. "Captain Callahan, the rest of our secret orders can't be accessed without your personal code."

"Oh . . . yes . . . sorry, I was caught up in my thoughts about the mission," the Captain replied haltingly.

"Yes sir, it's going to be a tricky one at best," Officer Bryant agreed. "But we've got a good crew, sir, the best!"

"That we have. Let's go and prepare them for what is to come," the Captain stated confidently as he strode toward the door with his head held high.

From all over the ship, the crews had gathered in the main briefing compartment to hear the Federation Council's orders and the tacticians' plans for the mission. Only the three young crewmembers of the Seeker knew what was about to be said.

The Captain stood on his podium and faced his crew with his hands behind his back. He was there as the Supreme Commander of the mission, and with that responsibility came the power of life and death. The audience was silent with expectation.

"Ladies and gentlemen, you have been observed, scrutinized and tested in every way that we know in order to prove that you are made of the right stuff. You must be space-worthy to your very innermost being. When you're alone and no one is watching, I must have total confidence that you'll behave as trained. Everyone must work with integrity, without hypocrisy. There is no excuse for anyone to try to be a hero—we work as a team. Yes, lives depend on each of you performing your assigned tasks without regard for your personal comfort and safety. The success of this mission lies in our working together, supporting one another."

The Captain continued, "Although you each are skilled in different areas, you must be of one mind, considering each other as more important than yourself. And be genuine—there is no room for hypocrites. When tension mounts, remember what God says in His Word: "A soft answer turns away wrath." Deal with internal problems before they reach me. Or I'll deal with them—and you may not like the outcome. If anyone has an "I'm better than you are" attitude, that person is not flying in space as part of a team. Your actions will prove what you are made of!

Captain Callahan paused a moment and then continued to speak, "As to the mission, the Command Center has received a communiqué from a group of renegade asteroid explorers calling themselves the "Turf Takers." They turned against the mining companies that funded them, and they're nothing more than space pirates as far as I'm concerned. After attacking supply ships and some of the settlements on Mars and Titan, they have established a colony where they are holding our kidnapped scientists. They will become a worse threat if they can force the scientists who were kidnapped to work for them. Hence, the purpose of this mission is to get our people back."

"Tactical, take it from here," the Captain said, looking in the direction of the Weapons Officer.

"All right, listen up!" the tall, steely-eyed Weapons Officer barked with his eyes full of fire. "The Seeker team is going to make a high polar insertion from the far side of the quadrant. They will be moving faster than any ship has ever traveled, and in stealth mode. At first we will act as a decoy and come in where the pirates expect us. The sensors now installed on the Seeker are the finest in the universe, and they will probe for life signatures among the possible hiding places in the asteroid belt. Anything larger than a couple of centimeters that moves will be noted. Armed with our new and powerful offensive weapons, we will act as protector for the Seeker. She has only defensive systems aboard in order to make room for her power plant and sensor array. Captain."

"Thank you. Okay, Tactical and Navigation, you meet with the crew of the Seeker. I want to see Spec Ops and Maintenance in Briefing Room One on the double." Captain Callahan winked at Andrew, Jennifer and Cody and whispered, "Okay, let's go bring them home!"

The orbital loop would be easily performed because of Andrew's piloting skills. He was just a bit nervous about being zipped up in a plastic bag and covered with green slime for a week or so.

"If only there was some way I could avoid the goo!" moaned Andrew.

Jennifer giggled. "You're going to look like . . . well . . . like . . . ."

"Don't start this, Jen. It's not funny," Andrew said sternly.

After the briefings everyone seemed confident about the mission. The plan was to launch into the unknown tomorrow after the chapel service. Although it was a long day of careful planning, everyone seemed confident about the mission—and their jobs. The Captain had challenged them to do their jobs with integrity and to work as a team. Even Trey and his friends seemed to be taking their mandate more seriously.

I'm bushed! The training officers had us going through all kinds of procedures. It seems like we have done everything at least 100 times or more. Anyway, everyone listened when Captain Callahan gave us a lecture about integrity. For a minute I was wondering why we Cadets needed that speech—and then I saw Trey and his buds. I'm sure glad they were there to hear it. If you ask me, Trey is the biggest hypocrite on the ship—he always thinks he is better than someone else. But he's not. The Captain says that I'm better than he is . . . uhhh . . . speaking of hypocrites . . . do I sound like one, too? I'd better pray about that!

Later,

Cody

As a matter of fact, Cody does sound a little like a hypocrite. But what made him sound like one? Any time we find ourselves having the "I'm better than you are" attitude, we are in danger of becoming a hypocrite or a fraud. When we live our lives with integrity, we will not pretend to be better than others. for example, we will not pretend to be more spiritual than our other Christian friends. Rather, we will demonstrate truthfulness and humility. Being honest in our assessment of how God views us and others is the key to living without hypocrisy.

God has much to say to you this week as you study a very important part of the Bible, the Sermon on the Mount. In it you will find Jesus' teaching on hypocrisy and some practical ways to avoid it. You will know how God wants you to minister to others, what it means not to judge others and how to relate to your enemies. A wise person discerns what is good and evil with a humble, servant-like attitude. The Bible says that we are to examine ourselves. How about you? Do you sometimes sound like a hypocrite? If you do, this week's lessons are for you!

Cadet Challenge 17.1

1 Samuel 16:7

1. Fill in every other word in Box A. Check your Bible and make corrections.
2. Read your verse, then cover Box A and fill in every other word in Box B.
   Again correct any errors and study the verse.
3. Cover Boxes A and B and fill in all the words. Correct any errors.

A

But _____ Lord _____ to _____, "Do _____
look _____ his _____ or _____ the _____ of
_____ stature, _____ I _____ refused _____.
For _____ Lord _____ not _____ as ____ man _____, for
_____ looks _____ the _____ appearance, _____, the
_____ looks _____ the _____."

B

_____ the _____said _____ Samuel, "_____ not
_____ at _____ appearance _____ at _____ height _____
his _____, because ____ have _____ him. _____ the
_____ does _____ see _____ a _____sees, _____
man _____ at _____outward _____, but
_____Lord _____ at _____ heart."

C

_____ _____ _____ _____ _____ _____ _____ _____, "____
_____ _____ _____ _____ _____ _____ _____ _____ _____
_____ _____ _____ _____ _____ _____ _____.
_____ _____ __ _____ _____ _____ _____.
_____ _____ _____ _____ _____ _____ _____ _____
_____ ___ _____/ _____ _____ _____ _____ _____
_____ _____ _____ _____/ __
_____ _____ _____ _____ _____ _____."

Cadet Challenge 17.2

Do You Have the Right "BE" Attitude?

Using logic, match the phrases in the box to each Beatitude. Then use your Bibles to check your answers, correcting any mistakes.

Matthew 5:1-12

And seeing the multitudes, He went up on a mountain, and when He was seated His disciples came to Him. Then He opened His mouth and taught them, saying:

Blessed are . . .   For . . .

v. 3 the poor in spirit, _____

v. 4 those who mourn, _____

v. 5 the meek, _____

v. 6 those who hunger and thirst for
    righteousness, _____

v. 7 the merciful, _____

v. 8 the pure in heart, _____

v. 9 the peacemakers, _____

v. 10 those who are persecuted for
    righteousness' sake, _____

vs. 11-12 you when they revile and
    persecute you, and say all kinds of
    evil against you falsely for My sake, _____

they shall be called sons of God.	great is your reward in heaven,	they shall be comforted.
they shall obtain mercy.	they shall see God.	theirs is the kingdom of heaven.
they shall inherit the earth.	theirs is the kingdom of heaven.	they shall be filled.

Write out the exhortation in Verse 12.

_____

_____

_____

A Look Back

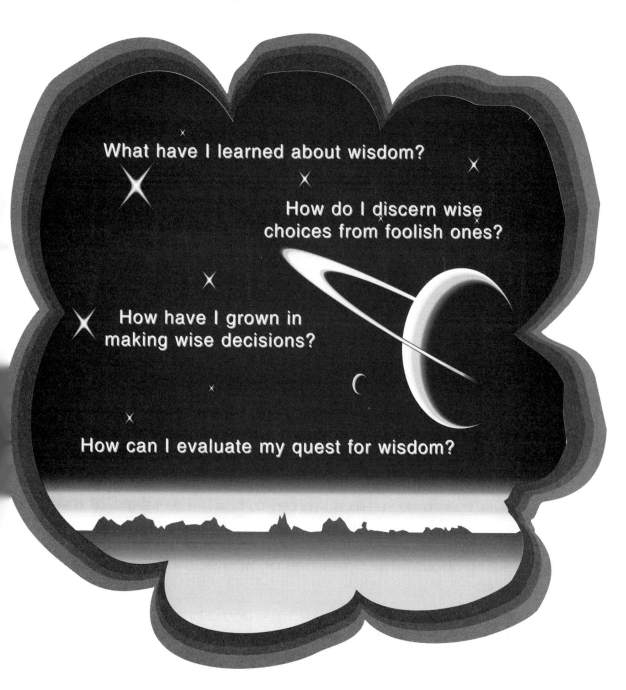

What have I learned about wisdom?

How do I discern wise choices from foolish ones?

How have I grown in making wise decisions?

How can I evaluate my quest for wisdom?

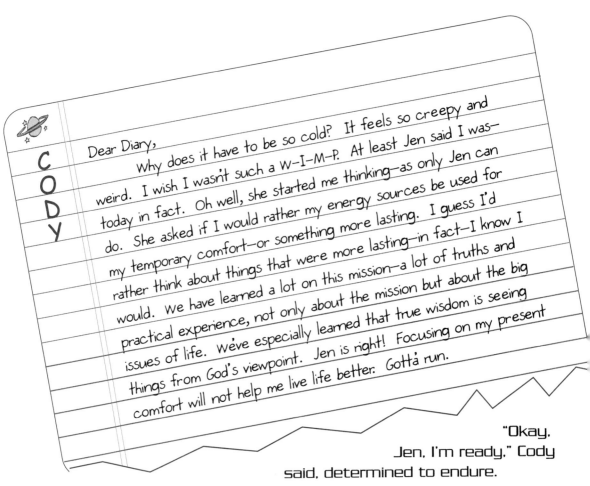

Dear Diary,

Why does it have to be so cold? It feels so creepy and weird. I wish I wasn't such a W-I-M-P. At least Jen said I was—today in fact. Oh well, she started me thinking—as only Jen can do. She asked if I would rather my energy sources be used for my temporary comfort—or something more lasting. I guess I'd rather think about things that were more lasting—in fact—I know I would. We have learned a lot on this mission—a lot of truths and practical experience, not only about the mission but about the big issues of life. We've especially learned that true wisdom is seeing things from God's viewpoint. Jen is right! Focusing on my present comfort will not help me live life better. Gotta run.

C
O
D
Y

"Okay, Jen, I'm ready," Cody said, determined to endure.

"Good! Now, just relax, Cody. Pretend you're being slimed by your classmates like you were at your graduation party. You really looked a mess then, although this is really different since we're inside the membrane."

Just then the pressure started to build. The weight of the fluid was pressing all over them in their acceleration-deceleration cylinders. The fluid-filled cylinders were their only means of surviving the physical pressure about to be unleashed on Seeker, their experimental space ship.

Cody's train of thought was interrupted briefly as he remembered how his grandfather, Fleet Admiral Haynes, had named the ship right before he sent them on their mission to rescue their parents from space pirates.

154

"Cody, concentrate!" Jen encouraged as she noticed Cody staring into space.

"Oh, sorry," Cody replied.

Since speed was important during the next phase, Andrew and Cody programmed the ship at max thrust. At the mid-course maneuver, the ship would flip 180 degrees and begin blasting against their forward momentum to slow them down.

"Guardian to Seeker. Do you copy?" barked the com. "We have no sensor readings of traffic in this sector whatsoever. You're clear to use maximum departure thrust, and no one will ever see you leave."

The aft section of the ship started to vibrate as the powerful fuel pumps began transferring the experimental fuels to the chambers. Technically, on an ordinary ship they'd be called combustion chambers, but this new triple combination of fuels, Tri-odek, was injected into a waiting nuclear plasma field. The process was the closest thing to total energy conversion that scientists could invent— almost like the merging of matter and anti-matter.

"Good night, guys," Cody nervously joked. "I'll see you in my dreams. Remember that our initial thrust will put us all in suspended animation for a time. But it will pass shortly."

"Sweet dreams!" they answered. Andrew and Jennifer were already covered, and were linked only by the communicators embedded in the membrane.

The swirling patterns of color looked like a kaleidoscope, and soon they seemed to be in dreamland.

The small ship, hurtling along at unimaginable velocities impossible only a few decades ago, blasted a tunnel through space up into the ecliptic. The Guardian, plodding along under the thrust of its massive drive engines, would take the more conventional route, serving as a decoy to fool the pirates into thinking that she was alone.

Cody closed his eyes as he remembered his parents' encouragement during his early days at the Academy. He was the youngest Cadet the Space Academy had ever accepted—and had ever graduated. With that last thought he was gradually wafted into a gentle sleep, and the violence of the engines slipped into the background.

The mission was on the mind of each Cadet when they drifted off. Andrew, being the oldest, felt responsible for the family now that his parents were missing. His mom had designed their experimental ship—and he was determined to use it to rescue them from the pirates. Over the past few months, Andrew had reflected on their initial launch for Earth's space station Orion. He had grown to respect his crewmates, even Trey and his buds who did not live for the Lord.

In a thoughtful analogy, Andrew compared the ship's Operating Manual to the Bible. Just as the whole crew had learned to trust the carefully drafted manual in repairing the space station, the Cadets had learned to have faith in God and His Word. Scripture had been proven true and powerful in his own life.

Jennifer, although a little too serious, was a great engineer. Her responsibilities involved the defense of the ship. She knew the Seeker inside and out—even as well as her brothers did. As she fell asleep, her dreams were mostly about family and the love they shared. The revelation that the Fleet Admiral was really their grandfather motivated all of them. The Admiral had become totally personable and approachable. It reminded her of Christ's incarnation—how He became flesh to show us what God is really like.

As Cody drifted into his sleep stage, he thought of the wisdom he'd gained while working with the others. He wanted to be a modern-day Daniel—no matter what the consequences. Cody was already born-again just like Jesus had told Nicodemus. But now he wanted to understand how he could allow the Holy Spirit to give him the power he needed to not be so afraid. He remembered how Jen and Andrew encouraged him to be more like Gideon. He wondered how he could guard his speech and avoid the tendency to say things that displeased God. He wondered how he could learn to praise Him more. Cody made the wise decision to live wisely and to not be distracted by others less committed to the Lord.

This was a very complicated and challenging mission. Using the stealth mode, they would navigate between asteroids, land on one of Jupiter's moons and set up surveillance to locate the patrol routes used by the pirates as they chased the Guardian, which was acting as their decoy.

Cody didn't want to think about the dangerous part. He was already scared just remembering that he was inside a giant tube of green slime. If only he could wake up and wash!

Suddenly, the violence of the engine ceased and the gentle bumping of the steering jets nudged them awake. They had arrived, and had not been seen by anyone! But exactly where were they? The protective gel drained, and Andrew was the first to dash to the control room to check the ship's status.

"Systems all green," Andrew reported with relief. "How about our position, Cody—any luck with the coordinates?"

"Great job!" Cody complimented Andrew. "Jennifer, is our defensive sensor array out full?"

"All set, guys," Jennifer answered confidently. "Let's settle down and see what's out there. We can remain undetected as long as we need to in this mode. The Lord has sure been good to us. What a comfort to know He's also watching over Mom and Dad, as well as Captain Callahan and the crew of the Guardian and us! Now our mission really begins in earnest."

"Yeah, as soon as I get this slime out of my ears," Cody muttered to himself.

What a day! We were totally undetected—and we are that much closer to rescuing Mom and Dad. The "gentle sleep phase," as Jen called it, was weird. I dreamed of spiritual things, mainly. Wow! I wish I could do that all the time—then maybe I wouldn't have night-mares. When I told Jen about it, she said she hoped that was evi-dence of me maturing in the Lord and gaining His wisdom. Actually, I think she's right—I think I am growing in my spiritual quest for wisdom, because I know God better than before I began the mission. I'm beginning to think about the consequences of my decisions before acting on them.

Later,

Cody

How does Cody know that he is gaining wisdom? If you said "because he is beginning to think about the consequences of his decisions before he acts on them," you are right. Thinking ahead about the consequences of your choices is wise thinking. If you are asking God for directions, then obeying His commands and using discernment about which decisions are wise and which ones are unwise, you are growing in wisdom. This week we will review the truths we have discussed in Bible class over the past 17 weeks. So get ready! You will be amazed at all you have learned in your own quest for God's wisdom.

Cadet Challenge 18.1

#1

Verse: _____

_____

_____

Why? _____

#2

Verse: _____

_____

_____

Why? _____

#3

Verse: _____

_____

_____

Why? _____

Cadet Challenge 18.2

Which Lesson Helped You the Most?

Fill in the blanks:

The lesson that helped me the most was _____

_____.

The reason that it helped me was _____

_____

_____

I would like to gain wisdom in the areas of _____

_____

_____

I need wisdom in those areas because _____

_____

_____

I can gain wisdom in those areas if I will _____

_____

_____